SHOWING SECRETS

SHOWING SECRETS

The Ultimate Guide to
Showing Horses and Ponies

CAROLYN HENDERSON

J. A. Allen

In memory of Face the Music, a top show horse and a great friend –
and with thanks to Marie and Tracey Parish, who entrusted
him to me for the last years of his life.

© Carolyn Henderson 2003

First published in Great Britain 2003
Reprinted 2004

ISBN 0 85131 789 8

J.A. Allen
Clerkenwell House
Clerkenwell Green
London EC1R 0HT

J.A. Allen is an imprint of Robert Hale Ltd

British Library Cataloguing in Publication Data
A catalogue record for this book is available from the British Library

Edited by John Beaton
Design by Judy Linard
Colour separation by Tenon & Polert Colour Scanning Ltd
Printed in Singapore by Kyodo Printing Co (S'pore) Pte Ltd

CONTENTS

ILLUSTRATIONS

All photographs unless otherwise credited are the copyright of John Henderson and are reproduced by his permission.

The diagram on page 106 is reproduced fron *The Horse Shoeing Book* by Martin Humphrey (J. A. Allen, 1995).

ACKNOWLEDGEMENTS

As anyone involved with horses knows, doing it by the book sometimes only works if the horse has read that particular manual. However, the difference with *Showing Secrets* is that a lot of talented producers and riders have been prepared to share some of those hard earned lessons. Thanks are due to them all, but a few in particular deserve special mention.

Lynn Russell is best known for producing many of the country's top cobs, but her ability to spot potential show horses of all types – and make the most of them – is legendary. Spending a day at her showing and dealing yard in Surrey makes you appreciate that if you want success, you have to work for it: I don't know anyone who works harder.

Kate Moore is another multi-talented rider and producer who has a special gift for understanding and educating young horses. The Essex yard she runs with her parents, Mike and Jill Jerram, is only ever full of happy horses.

Team Hollings combine expertise in all aspects of showing, from show ponies to Arabs. From their Lancashire base, they have produced champions of all sizes and know how to get the best from riders as well as ponies and horses.

Julia Woods, known to many as Julia Spacey Woods, is the best possible ambassador for Britain's native breeds and always keeps her enthusiasm and sense of humour. She has broken and produced numerous top class ponies at her Suffolk yard, particularly Connemaras.

Lynda Lodge, chairman of the British Skewbald and Piebald Association, is a dedicated champion of the coloured horse and pony. She and Sandra Lawrence, her partner in Wulfstan Stud, Cambridgeshire, have worked tirelessly to raise standards and promote enjoyment in showing.

The author is grateful to the British Skewbald and Piebald Association for permission to reproduce their copyright material on page 24.

FIRST WORD

Showing is one of the most fascinating and fun ways to enjoy your horse or pony. Over the past ten years, it has expanded into a world that has something for everyone, whether you own a potential Horse of the Year Show working hunter champion, a coloured horse, a show pony or a native. Once thought of by those in other disciplines as just an equine beauty contest, it is now recognized not just as a demanding competitive sphere in its own right but as a shop window for the breeding and production of sound, correct animals that are true to their types or breeds.

Many people become so hooked on showing, with all its fascinations and frustrations, that they become specialists. Others use it as a valuable part of their horses' education, as it is a great way to get a youngster used to the sights and sounds of the competition world and to behave in company, or as another way of having fun with an all-rounder who perhaps also does dressage and show jumping.

As the popularity of showing has grown, so the standards of production and presentation have risen. Competition gets hotter every season and even at local level you need to make the most of your horse or pony in every way to be at the top of the line. Increased interest means increased demand for potential stars, but although top animals can and do change hands for big money, you don't have to win the lottery to get to the top. If you have £20,000 to go out and buy a ready-made rosette machine, you can, but unless you have the knowledge, dedication and ability to carry on producing and riding it to the same high standards, you will not get the same results. In any case, one of the main attractions for many enthusiasts is the dream of finding a star in the rough. Without devaluing the role of the schoolmaster, many people get far more satisfaction from spotting and nurturing potential than from buying the finished product. That does not mean, of course, that you cannot get just as much fulfilment from progressing with a novice who has been correctly introduced to showing…or even, if you are a particularly patient and talented rider, taking on a horse who has 'gone wrong' and putting it back on the right lines.

When you look at reports and results from the big shows, it is usually the professionals who consistently head the line-ups. But although they dominate the top levels, they do not have it all their own way – and despite the oft-heard grumbles, good judges do not judge riders rather than horses. It is more a case that a professional will present a horse well and give the judge every chance to see its way of going; if a horse goes badly under saddle or plays up when asked to trot out in hand, it will lessen or even ruin its chances. A judge has to make his or her decision on what is there, not on what might be there if the horse behaves itself or is shown off to better advantage.

Having said that, an amateur with professional standards can and will stand an equal chance of heading the line. In some circumstances, such an owner may even have an advantage, particularly if he or she owns just one horse and has the time to concentrate on it to the exclusion of all else. The best professional yards treat their horses as individuals, but there have been cases where professionals have sold horses because they did not fit into busy set-ups or needed more time to mature than was economically viable, only to be beaten by the new owner a couple of years down the line.

Unless you aim to make showing part of your living, either by producing horses for sale and using the show ring as a shop window or by keeping and competing horses at livery, you will be doing it for fun. In any case, even the professionals have to enjoy what they do or they simply would not do it: there are easier ways of making a living than getting up at an unearthly hour and spending long days on showgrounds, let alone doing all the work behind the scenes. Doing it for fun and at the same time to the best of your ability does mean that you have to set your standards high; competition is fierce, albeit hopefully friendly.

The showing world is not a selfish one and no matter how businesslike an approach they take to it, all successful riders take a pride in their horses and ponies. Whatever area interests you, you will find that people love to talk about their animals. As long as you ask them at the right way and in the right time, those who succeed will nearly always be happy to advise those who are starting out. The professionals and others whose advice is passed on in these pages were all happy to pass on tips, techniques and opinions, even if they had to learn the hard way! Although they are well-known names, they all had to start somewhere. The judges quoted are also people with a wealth of experience and have either competed successfully or are still doing so, and know what it is like on both sides of the fence. In many cases the advice offered applies to ponies as well as horses, so chapters look at general areas such as tack and schooling then branch into special considerations for different types of animal where necessary.

Whether you are hoping to start showing, either with a horse or pony you own already or one bought specifically for the job, or want to improve on your current performance, you will find plenty of inspiration in this book. I can't guarantee that after you've read it, you'll be able to find a potential Wembley cob by spotting a hairy prospect in a field or re-schooling a badly behaved horse that other people have given up on, as Lynn Russell has done on several occasions. Nor can I offer good odds that you can follow Kate Moore's example and turn a former racehorse into a champion hack or produce a perfect pony to rival those in the Hollings team. But then again, you just might.

Horses and certainties rarely go together, but the one promise I can make is that with hard work, dedication and enthusiasm you will have a lot of fun and enormous satisfaction. Welcome to the world of showing.

Author's Note – Heights used in this book

Where references are given to height, you will sometimes find them given in hands and inches and in the metric equivalent – for example, 14.2hh and 148cm. This is because although societies such as the British Show Hack, Cob and Riding Horse Association have gone metric, many readers may prefer to have the equivalent traditional measurement for reference. The situation is complicated as some classes, such as the hunter weight divisions, have no height restrictions and if a horse's height is discussed it is still referred to in hands and inches. Also, whilst some breed societies – notably those for native ponies – have adopted metric measurements, others have stuck with hands and inches.

1 STARTING OUT

Many people first become interested in showing by having a go at local level with a horse or pony they already own. As long as it has good conformation and movement and is a decent performer, they may well be successful – perhaps, if the horse fits into a specific category or is a good example of its breed, successful enough to compete and win at larger shows. However, riders who are aiming high or thinking of buying an animal specifically for a ridden show career need to decide where their interests lie and what sort of horse or pony would be suitable.

Show horses can be just as versatile as any other. Whilst the professional with the absolutely top class horse will not usually be interested in competing in other spheres, the amateur owner/rider will often want to enjoy dressage, show jumping or other activities. Having said that, professionals know that one of the secrets of keeping a show horse sweet is to give it a variety of work without taking unnecessary risks. Most will hack out regularly; some of the best cobs and hunters are jumped and even hunted and many ponies, especially the show hunter and show hunter types, compete in dressage, show jumping and cross-country competitions. Show jumping and gridwork is a natural part of the regime for those who compete in workers' classes and hack and riding horse owners who compete for pleasure often do dressage as a sideline. Apart from the basic requirements of conformation and movement (see chapter 4) the show horse has two essential qualities which may make the difference between winning and losing. One is that it is true to type or breed: it must fit its particular category or breed specifications. The other is that it must have presence, a natural sparkle that says 'Look at me' when it is going round the ring with twenty others.

Another consideration, especially for the amateur exhibitor who may only keep one or two horses and looks after them either at home or on a DIY livery yard, is temperament. A horse can be bright and sensitive, but still have the sort of temperament that makes it easy to work with – provided, of course, that its rider has the necessary ability. Difficult horses, particularly those with a tendency to nap or whose reply to every question is 'I don't think I want to, so what are you going to do about it?' may need a professional to persuade them to change their attitude. Ninety-nine times out of a hundred, difficult horses have been made that way through bad handling or riding, are in discomfort or pain that has not been recognized, or are uneducated. If you have plenty of patience and enjoy a challenge, you might be the one to succeed where others have failed, but if you want to avoid problems it is usually best to find a horse who is more straightforward.

The basic types of show horse – ponies are looked at in the next chapter – are hunters, hacks, cobs and riding horses, with further divisions of height or weight-carrying ability between each type. One of the best ways to appreciate the character-istics of each is to study the animals who regularly win at top level; look at the overall picture, from conformation and way of going to turnout and ring technique. Some of our leading exhibitors also take part in lecture demonstrations where live 'models' are provided, and these can be entertaining as well as educational.

Perhaps one of the most difficult, but also one of the most essential, things to do is to be realistic. It's too easy to fall in love with an elegant hack which floats round the ring, or a middleweight hunter powering into its gallop, without thinking of the whys and wherefores of keeping and producing them yourself, especially if your horse is on a DIY livery yard or at home with limited facilities. If you've really set your heart on such a horse, then nothing will persuade you otherwise – and there is nothing to stop you having a go. For example, Silent Word, a very successful Thoroughbred show hack, was bought out of training by her owners as a three-year-old and when she won at the British Show Hack, Cob and Riding Horse Association's national championships was being schooled on the South Downs, with a regular audience of sheep! This partnership works because the mare belongs to a dedicated family which has a wide experience and knowledge of TBs and includes very capable riders. If you can't match this sort of knowledge and ability, you might be better thinking in terms of a small hunter, a cob or a riding horse.

Do not make the mistake of thinking that native ponies are only for children. The large breeds can and do perform in every sphere with adults and, like coloured horses, are enjoying a boom in popularity. Veteran showing classes are another area which is becoming increasingly popular and anything which encourages interest in the physical and mental welfare of older animals has to be a good thing.

At the end of the day, you have to want to see your horse or pony's head over the stable door every morning, even when it is dark, freezing cold, pouring down with rain and the show season seems light years away. For your horse's sake, you also want to know that he's equally glad to see you – so it is worth doing everything possible to make sure your choice is the right one.

This chapter looks at the four classic types of show horse – hunters, hacks, cobs and riding horses – whilst the next chapter focuses on show and native ponies, coloured horses, breed classes and veterans. There is no suggestion that the one group is in any way superior to another, as it's very much a case of horses for courses. There are also areas which may cross over; for instance, a skewbald or piebald cob may show equally well in show cob and coloured classes and an Anglo or part-bred Arab may also excel as a show hack.

Hunters

Hunters are sometimes described as the elite of the show ring and certainly a top quality show hunter will always find a ready buyer at a substantial price. It used to be said that this was not a class for the amateur, but although the top accolades usually go to professionals, there are plenty of amateurs ready to take them on and classes introduced specifically for amateur owner/riders are producing combinations that can hold their own in any company.

Traditionally, the three weight classes – lightweight, middleweight and heavyweight – and are the most prestigious. There are also sections for small hunters, ladies'

Lynn Russell with Bailey's Pukka Tukka, a novice lightweight hunter

hunters to be ridden astride or side-saddle and working hunters, plus classes for novice animals with limited winnings and those owned by amateur owner/riders. The basic definitions of the weight classes are:

> *Lightweight* – a horse that can carry up to 12st 7lb
> *Middleweight* – a horse that can carry 12st 7lb to 14 stone
> *Heavyweight* – a horse that can carry 14 stone and over.

Unfortunately, the trouble with basic definitions is that real life is not always that simple. One of the highest compliments a judge can pay is to say that a horse is a true representative of its weight division; plenty of nice animals hover between one category and the next, which makes things difficult. A 'light middleweight' might be outside the lightweight class, but lack the depth or substance of the true middleweight. In this case, it could perhaps show as a ladies' or working hunter if weight class results prove disappointing. At one time, lightweight hunters sometimes appeared to be taller than was needed. As the late Lady Zinnia Judd, a respected producer and judge, pointed out, the average rider of up to 12st 7lb does not need a 17hh (173cm) horse. Many agree with her and there now seem to be fewer giraffes in lightweight classes.

Ladies' hunters should be suitable to carry a lady out hunting and are therefore likely to be lightweights or middleweights at the lower end of that category. There are classes for ladies' hunters to be ridden astride and also side-saddle, which is a speciality in its own right.

Noble Clover, Kate Moore's novice heavyweight and working hunter

Bailey's Over Ice, shown successfully as a small hunter and later equally successful in intermediate classes

Small hunters might not claim the main ring priority given to weight classes and rarely get the chance to take part in major championships, which are usually contested only by winners and reserves in the weight classes. However, they have gained an enormous popularity and are extremely versatile; from the amateur owner's point of view, they can do just about any other activity and if decent jumpers, can compete on equal terms with larger horses in working hunter classes. They are defined not by their weight carrying ability but by their height; they must be over 148cm but not exceed 158cm. It is important that they are horses as opposed to overgrown ponies, and the ideal small hunter is a miniature middleweight. It must still be able to carry most adults, which means that it must have substance as well as quality and be deep enough through the girth to take all but the tallest rider's leg. Working hunters should have all the attributes of a show hunter, with the added ability to jump a course of 'natural' fences in a bold, flowing, rhythmic style. Fence heights vary, as do the difficulty of courses, and range from 76cm (2ft 6in) or even less at local level to 107cm (3ft 6in) plus at county shows. You will find that course builders' definitions of 'natural' fences vary: some stick to a straightforward interpretation of the word whilst others have been known to include mind-boggling extras, such as a pen of sheep sited near a fence!

Larger shows may divide workers into lightweight and heavyweight divisions, but many make no distinction. In either case, it offers a good opportunity to the horse who has a decent jump and perhaps falls between two weight divisions for the straight showing classes.

THE EXHIBITOR'S VIEW

A hunter should combine quality and substance. It must be workmanlike rather than elegant but never common and, like all show horses, give a really good ride. You want to feel that you could have a really good day's hunting on it without having to leg it on all the time to keep it going, or feeling as if your arms are going to be pulled out. It should be up to the bridle without leaning on your hands and cover the ground. A hunter must be able to gallop, but it must come back to you afterwards – you sometimes see riders with fixed smiles on their faces desperately trying to disguise the fact they are being rather tanked off with! It can be quite funny to watch, but remember that being out of control in the hunting field is a cardinal sin. Small hunters can give you a lot of fun. When I'm looking for one, or trying to decide if a horse would fit into that category, I always ask myself: Is it the perfect pattern of a miniature middleweight?

A hunter must always strike you as just that. If the judge has to look twice to decide whether it's a hunter or a riding horse, it probably isn't a good example of either. Young horses mature, of course, and it isn't unusual for one to start out as a lightweight and end up as a middleweight. You just have to keep your fingers crossed that it ends up as one or the other, not somewhere between the two.

Lynn Russell, show producer

A JUDGE'S VIEW

Some people think that if their horse is between classes – say it's more than a lightweight but not quite a true middleweight – they can disguise this and boost it into the next category by putting weight on it. I'm afraid they are conning themselves; apart from the fact that the message that an overweight horse is being put under too much stress is getting through at all levels, part of the art of being a judge is to see what's really there.

As for height, I wouldn't say that biggest is always best, though obviously judges have different opinions. Personally, I don't like to see 17hh lightweights because this usually means that the sort of rider they are meant to carry would need a step ladder to get on. Some horses naturally 'ride big' and I prefer this to a tall horse which gives you the impression that you're sitting on something a hand smaller. I also hate clumsy horses, because the last thing you want in the hunting field is a horse that falls over its own feet.

Sally Hennessy on the ladies' hunter Rosenburg

I don't care whether a horse is a mare or a gelding and I try not to take colour into account. I have my own preferences, as does everyone, but I would never put, for example, a bay horse above a chestnut simply because I preferred its colour. There was a ridiculous letter in one of the equestrian magazines recently from an exhibitor claiming that her horse had been ignored by the judge because it was chestnut – her reasoning was that because it and the other three chestnuts in the class were down the line, the judge was prejudiced against this colour. She obviously had not thought to ask herself if it might simply be that none had the conformation, movement or ride to warrant being higher up the line!

Someone asked me once if I would give a coloured horse (a piebald or skewbald) equal consideration with solid coloured ones and in all honesty, I would. Of course, it would have to be up to the same standards of conformation, type, movement and ride. In one way it was a hypothetical question, as I haven't yet had a coloured hunter before me in straight show classes, though I have seen several do very well in working hunter classes. I always remember seeing Lady Zinnia Judd choose a 15hh coloured horse as her winner in a county workers' class and thinking how wonderful it was that she judged what she saw before her and was not hidebound by tradition.

Cobs

Cobs have enjoyed an enormous and deserved rise in popularity over the past few years, as more and more riders realize how versatile they are and how much fun they have to offer. From the amateur rider's point of view, they can do anything from dressage to show jumping as well as showing; several cobs have 'retired' from the show ring and gone on to be successful in affiliated show jumping up to Foxhunter level. They can be equally at home in the dressage arena: Milkyway, a former Wembley Cob of the Year, and Percy Vere, Allister Hood's former successful lightweight, have both made successful career changes.

Their type means they are suitable for riders of just about any size and weight, and they are nearly always good doers – which makes them cheaper to keep than horses which need more hard feed. Because most cobs have a large percentage of draught blood, many are level headed and most have kind temperaments. However, it is a mistake to think that they are plods; some can be quite a challenge when in the peak of condition and if they have the necessary presence and sparkle to succeed in the show ring, they may well have a character and sense of humour to go with it.

The show cob must be over 148cm but not exceed 155cm. Classes are divided into lightweight and heavyweight sections and there are also classes for working cobs, which follow the same lines as those for working hunters. Again, there are classes specifically for novice animals and for those owned by amateur owner/riders. The good show cob is a definite type, with a quality but workmanlike head, powerful neck, deep body, relatively short legs and powerful back end. Many of the best have been accidents of breeding, though some breeders have taken up the challenge of trying to produce them and there are cob breeding classes along the same lines as those for other categories. Polaris, Lynn Russell's 1999 Cob of the Year and winner of the 2002 All-England Championship at Royal Windsor Horse Show, is a pure bred Irish Draught by Silver Jasper and the Irish Draught cross Connemara is also proving popular.

EXHIBITORS' VIEWS

The show cob is a riding animal, and so must have a good shoulder and good set of limbs to give a comfortable, well-balanced ride. It shouldn't clomp along like a driving cob would. You want a fairly low action, with not too much bend in the knee, and it must still have quality – a lot of not so good show cobs are really vanners with the feather trimmed off.

Robert Oliver, show producer

Draco, Lynn Russell's novice lightweight cob

If I could only have one show horse, just for my own pleasure, it would be a cob. If they are built, schooled and ridden correctly they can give you a ride as light and balanced as any other horse; too many people think it's acceptable for a cob to lean on the rider's hands because they don't appreciate that they can go any other way! A cob can do anything, astride or side-saddle. I've won concours d'elegance classes on my cobs and beaten what you would politely call the more accepted types. Most of them enjoy jumping and jump well.

You can do a lot with clever 'trimming and strimming,' but to show at decent level a cob has got to be correct. The old saying about a good cob is that it should have a head like a lady and a backside like a cook, which gives you the idea.

A cob must move from the shoulder with a good stride, not go up and down. Because of their build, they don't often have an extravagant walk, but you don't want a cob that waddles like a duck. A good, natural walk is an asset.

A horse with a good walk also has a good gallop, and that applies as much to cobs as to anything else. A cob, like a hunter, should be able to really let down and gallop, but come back to you when you ask.

Lynn Russell

A JUDGE'S VIEW

There are lots of nice cobs in the show ring, but the real stars are hard to find. Finding one who has the power and substance and the true cob characteristics coupled with quality is difficult; I see a lot of perfectly nice but common horses who have been clipped and trimmed within an inch of their lives but will never be true show cobs. You also see the occasional hunter type who has basically been stuffed with food until it is frankly fat – taking its mane off won't turn this sort of horse into a proper cob. As a type, cobs have deep bodies and short legs. However, this doesn't mean that they can't cover the ground. My pet hate is a cob who can't walk; I don't expect to see one move like a Grand Prix dressage horse, but there's no reason why a cob can't cover the ground.

It must also be able to gallop, and by that I mean sit down and really go. Some riders – and I can think of a few professionals as well as amateurs – have their cobs so fat that it's physically impossible for them to gallop. You must be given the distinct feeling that when the rider asks for gallop, the cob goes up another gear rather than just cantering faster.

I'm also very particular about a cob's limbs. These horses have to carry weight, and that means they must have good joints and good feet. I don't like long cannon bones and I don't like puffy joints. And whilst a cob has a relatively short, powerful neck compared to a hack or hunter, you must still feel that there is plenty in front of you. There's nothing worse than feeling that the horse's ears are in your mouth.

Hacks

Hacks are the most elegant of show horses and epitomize quality, elegance and grace. However, they must still have enough substance to carry the average adult rider. They are divided into small or large categories; small hacks are over 148cm but must not exceed 154cm and large hacks are over 154 cm but not exceeding 160cm.

There were originally two types of hack, park hacks and covert hacks. Covert hacks were basically safe conveyances for carrying riders to hunt meets, whilst park hacks were for poseurs who rode to be seen! It was said that a gentleman should be able to read his correspondence whilst riding his hack one-handed down London's Rotten Row, whilst a lady should be safe and supremely elegant in all circumstances.

Most hacks are Thoroughbred or near, or Anglo-Arab. Many successful ones have come out of racing, and although 'blood' horses are usually sensitive they are not necessarily difficult if re-schooled correctly and taken on by a rider who understands them. It is often said that they are not suitable for amateur owners, but there is no reason why the competent, dedicated one or two-horse owner who can give them individual attention should not be successful.

EXHIBITOR'S VIEWS

Ideally, the perfect hack is a Thoroughbred with soft, elegant movement and effortless natural carriage. It must be a very straight mover, with no knee action. I want to see a nice head with a generous eye and enough room to fit two fingers between the jaw and neck bone so it can flex the jaw with ease. There should be a good length of neck and the neck should not come out of the withers too low down. The back should not be too long or too short and there must be a good shoulder with a pronounced girthline, so the saddle sits naturally in the right place. I want a very correct foreleg, quite long in the forearm so it acts as a pendulum for quality movement.

Behind the saddle, I look for good, low set hocks – the horse is then able to use its hocks to assist in self carriage. The tail should be well set on.

One of the most important features of a top show hack is that magic ingredient of charisma. You can even see it in a horse that is in almost skeletal condition, but has that look about it; it's the sort of horse that even someone who knows nothing about them says 'Isn't that lovely'.

Having got all that, I hope it doesn't weave, crib bite, windsuck and isn't blind in one eye or has a terrible temperament! I can forgive them being house devils if they are street angels – you can put up with one that tries to bite you in the stable if it comes up with the goods in the ring. Manners are important, but these are not police horses and they're not deaf and blind. If a hole opened up in front of you, you wouldn't want it to fall in it and break its neck and yours!

There are still good hacks of true type and you can still find them and breed them, but there are too many veering towards riding horse type or with too much pony influence.

John Keen, exhibitor, breeder and judge

The hack has always been TB or near, but those of years ago definitely had more bone. People see an animal with no bone and think it's a hack, but quality is not lightness of bone.

Hacks are meant to be ridden by an average sized adult, men and women. You often hear complaints that someone is too big to be judging or riding hacks, but remember that they were originally either covert hacks, ridden to the meet, or park hacks, to be seen on – and had to carry both sexes.

Ideally the hack is a small TB with good bone and depth of girth, but the TB itself has got lighter of bone: you only have to look at Flat horses. The hack should have quality with enough substance and bone, but in general we're not breeding TBs of that type, which is a great shame.

The large hack
City Lights, shown
by Kate Moore

Unfortunately, too, the modern show ring doesn't lend itself to the high couraged, top class show hack. You get all the sights and sounds, with bands, sponsors' banners, parachutists and whatever and whilst manners have always been important, no horse is bombproof.

Many hacks today are not taught to stand still and good manners are not instilled. It comes down to correct handling, being fair but firm and taking time. A hack wants time and miles on the clock – years ago people would take three seasons to produce one, now it's sometimes a matter of take it to a show or two, then to Wembley and blow its brains as a four or five-year-old.

There should be a real difference between a hack and a riding horse. A riding horse can be a stronger type and ride: if you ride a good hack, it is very light, effortless and elegant.

Robert Oliver, exhibitor and judge

The biggest problem is that people are not looking at the right type. They are going for horses that are either very ponyish or are basically weedy. A hack has got to have lots of quality, but it must still have the appropriate amount of substance. It's got to be able to carry a lady or a not too large man. You want it to be deep, with a good chest, a good shoulder and enough quality bone. The neck should be set on correctly and have a good turn, and the horse must have natural presence.

He's got to say 'Look at me'. That sort of horse is much easier to produce to sit up and go. Too many people fall for a pretty head and forget the rest – and whilst you don't want an overly plain head, remember that you can do a lot to dress it up with the right bridle. A pretty head isn't the top priority. Ride is vital. It's got to be light, with a good mouth; I don't want to feel that I'm being pulled downhill. The hack should move perfectly straight, flicking his toes and floating over the ground, and should flow through the changes of pace and have beautiful manners.

My personal preference, and it is very much a personal thing, tends towards the Thoroughbred. I don't particularly like too much Arab influence, as I feel it can make them look a bit 'twee'.

There are very few hacks with the quality, substance, movement and ride of the top class animal. A hack should carry itself through the shoulder and carry itself naturally without the rider having to organize it; on a really good one, you're sitting there effortlessly whilst it happens underneath you.

There are a lot of 'ponies' in the small hacks. The true hack was always the beautiful small TB with substance and movement, but a lot of people can't handle them. People don't seem to think that a hack should have sufficient limb, but this is essential for any horse in any discipline – or they think that because it has little light limbs, it's a hack. A lot of them are tied in below the knee, where the area immediately below the knee is too small and restricted and the tendons too small for the horse, which is a weakness. You also see too many horses which lack depth through the body and too much priority is placed on a pretty head.

A hack has got to be very elegant, but with enough substance. A riding horse should still have quality, but can be more workmanlike. Both should have presence, but a hack must ooze elegance. When you're riding a good hack, you should feel as if you're dressed in a beautiful ballgown and everyone else is wearing casuals!

Kate Moore, producer and judge

When the metric measurements came in, we raised the height of the small hacks so the maximum was 154cm, just over 15.1hh, instead of 15hh. This was to try and get rid of the 'pony element' and I think the type has improved. You don't get many 15hh TBs and to get the height down, you either get a bit of Arab or a bit of pony. I think people today don't realize what hacks are meant to be used for; a small hack should be able to carry twelve and a half stone, but of course you can only judge what's in front of you.

The large hack has got to be elegant; the set-on of head to neck to shoulder should be elegant. I do think we have some lovely hacks at the moment, though I agree that some are bordering on being riding horses. There is quite a narrow borderline between the two, but the riding horse should have a little more limb and the hack should be a more elegant, light mover. The hack should have a bit more extravagant trot, but the riding horse can have a slightly rounder action.

Jennifer Williams, breeder, exhibitor and former chairman of the British Show Hack,
Cob and Riding Horse Association

A JUDGE'S VIEW

A hack must be light in the hand and beautifully balanced. It must never, ever be strong, but unfortunately you do see some that are. I don't know if it's that there are fewer riders nowadays with the knowledge and ability to school a horse in self carriage, or that they don't appreciate the true characteristics of the hack. You have to remember, though, that this should be a supremely well mannered ride.

There have been a few controversies when judges have made their final line-up and then changed the placings because a horse has misbehaved or refused to stand. Personally, I would do exactly the same. I appreciate how deeply disappointing it must be for a rider if this happens, but you are on show until the final moment.

Conformation wise, I want to see an elegant horse, not a pretty, overgrown pony. Many successful hacks have been bred from the combination of a Thoroughbred stallion on a show pony mare, but they must still have 'horse' qualities.

Riding horses

Riding horse classes were originally introduced to fill a gap in the market. There are many top quality horses who are neither hunters nor hacks, but fall between the two categories – and because of their good conformation and movement, are still show horses. The riding horse is, as its name suggests, an animal you should feel you could happily ride for long periods at any pace over all sorts of terrain.

Classes are split into small and large sections. Small riding horses are over 148cm but not exceeding 158cm, whilst large riding horses are over 158cm but have no upper height limit. Some of the best riding horses of recent years have been Thoroughbreds or near with the all-important substance to match their quality, but part-bred Arabs and warmbloods have also made an impact.

THE EXHIBITOR'S VIEW

In many ways, the riding horse falls between the hack and the hunter, yet it should still be a definite type, with substance and quality. As its name suggests, it should

Kate Moore's small riding horse, Victoria Cross

be a pleasure to ride, comfortable and obedient, up to the bridle without being at all heavy. It should move straight and freely, though not flicking its toe as much as the show hack. A riding horse also has to gallop.

Kate Moore

A JUDGE'S VIEW

These can be some of the most difficult classes to judge, because you get quite a variation of horses. At top level, you usually find it easy enough to pick the ones that will head your line, but lower placings can be difficult and it comes down to personal preference. I suppose that's what judging is all about, but it doesn't make it any easier! When you see a really good riding horse, it can only be a riding horse, and that has to be the clincher. You might get horses that are very nice, but are really lightweight hunters that are being shown a bit leaner than they might be in their 'real' category or hacks that are not elegant enough. Personally, I'll move a horse up the placings if it gives a fantastic ride, because that's what it's all about. However, I wouldn't have a horse that was definitely more of a hack or hunter above a true riding horse unless the riding horse gave a bad ride.

2 OTHER OPTIONS

For many years, showing classes for horses were limited to hacks, cobs and hunters. Then a new section was introduced for the riding horse, because there were so many good quality, versatile horses which fell between the definitions of a hack and a hunter. At first, they were looked on as something of a novelty, but now the entries in these classes are as high in quality as they are in numbers.

These four categories are still looked on as being at the centre of the ridden showing world, but they have been joined by many others. Some, such as the breed classes, were once shown mainly in-hand but are equally popular under saddle whilst others, such as those for coloured horses and ponies, prove that the barriers of prejudice are all but broken down.

Different breeds will always have their devotees and whilst fashions change, there will always be people who would never consider buying anything other than, say, an Arab or a Welsh Cob. Whilst there have been many criticisms of breeders producing animals for the show ring rather than for their inherent qualities of characteristics – and perhaps losing qualities such as dense bone and hardiness in the search for a pretty head or a fashionably taller animal – it cannot be denied that showing keeps breeds in the public eye.

It also helps to dissolve prejudice. Even ten years ago, there were people who would rather ride a bike than a coloured horse, dismissing them as 'common gypsy horses'. Today, that attitude is almost unheard of and, coloured horses with good conformation and movement are much sought after, to the extent that if you stand a bay and a skewbald of equal merit side by side in a dealer's yard, the skewbald will inevitably have the higher price tag. They now have their own classes at the Horse of the Year Show and the Royal International Horse Show, under the auspices of the Coloured Horse and Pony Society and the British Skewbald and Piebald Association respectively.

The horse world has also woken up to the incredible versatility of the British native breeds; they have always been very popular in their regions of origin, but that has now spread nationwide and worldwide. Connemaras, for instance, have a huge following throughout the world, from Australia to New Zealand.

Breed classes

Classes for horses of a particular breed tend to be for animals shown in-hand rather than ridden. Notable exceptions are those for Arabians and part-bred Arabs – and, of course, for mountain and moorland ponies, which have a section of their own in the next chapter. Appaloosas and Quarter horses also have their own classes and their own shows. Pure-bred Arabians are viewed in a very narrow fashion in the showing world, which many Arab enthusiasts believe is unfair. They feel that there is no reason why an Arab could not be produced and shown successfully as a show hack or riding horse, particularly considering the modern show hack's origin as a horse to be seen on in fashionable society – and what could be more eye-catching than a beautifully schooled Arab?

When you see a well-schooled Arab in total harmony with its rider, you have to agree. Unfortunately, the standard of schooling and presentation of ridden Arabians does, on the whole, often fall below that of other categories of show horse. There are exhibitors who present as pleasing a picture as any producers of show hacks, and there are some beautifully schooled Arabians – but there are also some badly mannered horses and dire examples of turnout.

How much of the bad manners and poor way of going is down to the way many in-hand exhibitors encourage the Arabian's natural gaiety to the point of 'winding them up' is a subject that would provoke much discussion. There is also a big difference between the way Arabians and other breeds are encouraged to show themselves in-hand, though the exaggerated stretched stance seems to be not as popular or fashionable as it was and some vets have warned that it may even be a cause of sacroiliac injuries.

Anglo and part-bred Arabs have far greater showing opportunities, perhaps in part because they follow general turnout guidelines and are shown pulled and plaited; pure-bred Arabians are shown with full manes and tails. Many Anglos and part-breds are successful in hack and riding horse classes as well as breed ones and the Cherif championships for part-bred Arabs are hotly contested.

Although Appaloosas are a breed, most people think of them first and foremost in terms of colour. As with piebalds and skewbalds, there is, sadly, still prejudice against them – though signs are that it is gradually diminishing and they may, perhaps, be the next to see a surge in popularity.

Native ponies are on an ever-growing high and breed classes provide some of the largest numbers of entries at county level – see chapter 3.

A JUDGE'S VIEW

I'm afraid that in some cases, Arab horse owners have been their own worst enemy. There seems to be this feeling that they can't go on the bit and that we mustn't depress their gaiety and flamboyance. Well, if a horse is built correctly it can go on the bit just as nicely as any Thoroughbred; better than some, in fact, because Thoroughbreds are built to go long, low and fast.

There is also a definite difference between gaiety and bad manners. There is no excuse for a horse to jog instead of walk, or for it to refuse to stand still. The biggest problem can be trying to re-school a horse that has been hyped up in-hand, especially if it has been asked to stand stretched out. One of our top riders told me that she'd been asked to produce a successful in-hand horse under saddle, and her biggest problem was that it had to unlearn basic signals. Like most Arabs, it had been shown in an Arab slip with a chain under the jaw, and taught that pressure on the chain was a signal to raise its head. Now it was being ridden in a pelham and was having to learn that slight curb pressure was a signal to relax its jaw and come into a round outline. No wonder the poor horse was confused!

In theory, an Arab can fulfill the requirements of a hack or riding horse. In practice, I can't think of a single judge who would accept one as such. My own view is that the Arab is a supreme ridden horse that has its own niche and that exhibitors who want to go outside that would be better advised to ride an Anglo or part-bred.

One thing I would like to see is an improvement in facilities for ridden Arab classes. Rings are often small and sometimes unlevel, yet the classes often attract spectators because the horses are so attractive and flamboyant. There has been recent criticism of showing in the equestrian press by those who feel that it should be more of a 'spectator sport' with judges showing marks as they are awarded, perhaps by holding up cards as in the ice skating world.

Whether or not it would be a good idea to go that far is open to debate, but certainly there are ways to make show classes more interesting. And as Arabs are so lovely to look at, even if you know little about horses, it would be nice if more shows made more of them!

THE EXHIBITOR'S VIEW

I started showing because I wanted to do something just for fun. We'd got to Advanced Medium in dressage and though dressage is fun, it's hard work. We're amateurs, so horses are a hobby, but we do try and have professional standards on the yard.

Because the horse is such a lovely ride, and because he moves so well, we won right from the start in Appaloosa classes. He found it all quite easy, though that isn't meant to be big headed! Now I'm going to register him as a riding horse and, just for fun, see if we do meet any prejudice.

Mandy Southern, Appaloosa owner

Classes based on colour

Although the Appaloosa has a distinctive coat colouring based on a range of five recognized patterns, it is a breed. Palominos, piebalds and skewbalds, on the other hand, are colours and may be represented by many breeds and types. Some breed societies, such as the Welsh Cob, New Forest and Connemara, recognize palomino as a standard colour and an owner could therefore show such an animal in either category. However, coat colour would not be taken into consideration in a breed class, whilst for the horse to do well in palomino classes it would have to be an even colour – ideally that of a newly minted gold coin – with no more than 15 per cent dark hair in manes and tails. There are also definite rules as to what constitutes a coloured horse. If it only has white markings on the head, legs, belly and/or mane and tail in isolation, it is not classed as a skewbald or piebald. Clyde markings – long stockings and/or patches on the belly – are also insufficient to qualify. The white colour must be distributed in patches as opposed to spots.

Today you will find coloured (piebald and skewbald) warmblood horses, especially Dutch warmbloods, but the Hackney stud book is the only one which admits parti-coloured animals. Amongst native pony breeds, only Shetlands are 'allowed' to be skewbald or piebald – though as Edward Hart points out in *The Coloured Horse and Pony* (J A Allen), 'other breeds undoubtedly had them, including the Fell, New Forest and Welsh'.

Showing classes at large UK shows are held under the auspices of the Coloured Horse and Pony Society (CHAPS) or the British Skewbald and Piebald Society. The enormous popularity of coloured horses has been recognized by the establishment of CHAPS qualifying ridden classes for horses and ponies throughout the country for a final at the Horse of the Year Show, whilst the BSPA has its own qualifiers for a final at the Royal International Horse Show.

All the guidelines for conformation, movement and temperament apply as much to coloured horses as they do to other categories. However, because there is such a huge variety of types, it is important to be aware of what the judge is looking for. The following information comes from the BSPA's guidelines for judges of ridden finals at its national championships:

Because of the range, diversity and variety of breeding origins, i.e. Shetland to Shire, vanners to TB or warmblood, our ridden judges are required to place the greatest emphasis on ride, performance and manners. In addition, our classes also have children and junior riders competing against adults. Again, the emphasis is on ride and performance including the display as the all important criteria rather than either conformation or colour and markings. Colour and markings are of no significance other than as a last resort in achieving final placings, i.e. if all else is equal then judges are urged to use the visual effect of colour and markings as a final arbiter.

Clearly, conformation and being true to type is important but not to the exclusion of ridden performance. Again, if judges struggle to separate entries and to make final placings on ride, performance, manners, conformation etc then colour and marking can be used as the final arbiter.

The basic types are:

Warmbloods, British or Continental (Sports Horses)

These classes require a minimum of 25 per cent verifiable parentage and either BSPA 'blue papers' signifying verified parentage or other society breeding verification is required.

Thoroughbred types and crosses

Again, these types require verifiable breeding to a minimum standard of 25 per cent.

Hunters

This is a very popular class, entries being middleweight in general, enabling us to introduce a small hunter class for animals not exceeding 15.2hh.

Working hunters, ponies and cobs

These are judged with primary emphasis on jumping and style, which count for a possible 60 out of the overall 100 marks available. Conformation including type characteristics is up to 20 marks and ride and display is also up to 20 marks. We look, therefore, for the best jumping and performance horse/pony to come through rather than the prettiest.

Riding horse types

At the championships, riding horses are excluded from hunter classes and are expected to differentiate themselves from hack types. In open shows, such selectivity may not be required. Riding horses are judged on ride, manners and schooling and are asked to do an individual display including a gallop, ground conditions and safety considerations allowing. The judge should ride.

Cob/cob types

The range of types (draught/vanner and cross breeds) 'common' in skewbald and piebald cobs are frequently either riding or driving cob types and our national schedules have classes for both types. Ride and drive exhibits are also prevalent, hence our emphasis in ridden classes on the quality of the ride as distinct from just conformation. Cobs are entered as either lightweight or heavyweight. Lightweights should have at least eight inches of bone and be capable of carrying up to 14 stone. Heavyweights should have at least nine inches of bone and be capable of carrying over 14 stone. 'Super heavyweights' with bone exceeding $10\frac{1}{2}$ in are also prevalent.

Part-bred Arab/ American breeds and types and Hack types

This lightweight category includes the types which are finer and more flamboyant than either hunters or larger riding horses. The part-bred Arab is a popular cross and increasingly prevalent, along with the 'paint' and American types. The judging emphasis is on schooling, ride and display and judges should penalize exhibitors for lack of manners.

Vanners and Light Draughts

This cluster of types is very popular and includes many of the draught and driving animals. As with cob types and driving cobs, the vanner frequently displays the conformation characteristics of its draught origins, with cow hocks, upright shoulder or dishing not being uncommon. Judges are not as harsh on this as they would be in other type classes. All vanners should, however, be capable of displaying a very active and sharp trot, but in ridden classes may not always be able to extend or gallop as is expected of a riding cob or hunter. A vanner is frequently described as a typical tradesman's horse of pre-motor days of indiscriminate breeding. It is usually a hardy short-legged type (including light draught types).

When shown as a 'traditional,' the vanner is invariably a great eyecatcher, with mane, tail and feather flowing dramatically. However, not all traditionals are vanners, or indeed coldbloods.

British coldbloods

This is a broad category of types – cobs, vanners, natives, draughts – and as such is not a breed. Generally, they will be the indigenous horse or pony of the hardy, thrifty type for whom considerable trimming and clipping is required prior to showing unless the animal is being shown as a traditional.

Coldbloods will not have any Arab, Thoroughbred, warmblood and/or American blood in first or second generation sire or dam lines.

Traditionals

Traditional horses and ponies are so defined because of their manner of presentation. They are not a singular breed or type. Most, however, are of cob/vanner/draught origins, though by no means are they all British coldbloods. They must be presented with a full mane or tail, unplaited, and feathers untrimmed. Manes will be at least eight inches with feathering covering the coronet band on most of the foot.

Large British breeds and types

Types include Shire, Clydesdale, Suffolk and Irish Draught. As with the vanner and light draught classification, conformation features often – though not exclusively – include some draught features.

A JUDGE'S VIEW

The first question I always ask myself when looking at a coloured horse or pony is: Would I like it as much if it was a 'boring bay'? Colour and markings are obviously part of the attraction, but should never be given priority over the basics. We're trying to breed well-made, sound performers, not china ornaments.

Some people say that it's harder to assess the conformation of a coloured horse than one of solid colour, because the markings 'break up' the horse's outline. I agree that you may sometimes get optical illusions, but these can apply to solid coloured horses with white markings and a good judge should see the real picture. For instance, stockings can sometimes give the false impression that a horse is long in

The versatility of coloured horses, plus new championships, makes them increasingly popular

the cannon bone, whilst short socks can 'shorten' a cannon bone that is actually too long.

It's heartening to see that coloured horses are being accepted in straight showing classes and I think this trend will continue. There are some particularly nice riding ponies appearing and coloured cobs, of course, have long been accepted on an equal par. Personally, I think the riding horse barriers will be the next to be broken down, followed by hacks – an elegant coloured horse is delightful to look at and to ride and as more are being bred with a high percentage of Thoroughbred blood, the day of the skewbald show hack is perhaps not far away!

That is not meant in any way to detract from the traditional coloured cob with full mane, tail and feathers. It has many enthusiasts and if it meets high standards of conformation and movement is as good a horse as any other type. One of the attractions of the coloured horse world has always been its open mindedness and it would be sad if that disappeared and we started talking about 'right' and 'wrong' types.

Coloured working hunters have done and will continue to do well, but I think the show hunter classes will be the last bastion of prejudice to fall. There is little logic to this, when you think that the ideal hunter is often the draught cross Thoroughbred type, and the half-bred type coloured horse can often epitomize this. There is also the influence of the coloured warmblood, which cannot be denied.

A BREEDER AND SOCIETY ADMINISTRATOR'S VIEW

You only have to look at the success of our national show. For the past two years we have had around 250 horses and ponies of all types, all of which have qualified from previous shows.

For some people, one attraction of showing coloured horses lies in the wide variety of types. You have everything, from warmbloods and riding horse or hack types to traditionals, shown with flowing manes, tails and feather. Traditionals are becoming increasingly popular, which we're pleased about. The BSPA has always emphasized that the traditional is as good as any other horse and should not be 'put down' because of its hair. Indigenous stock was cold blooded, and you need to protect it. Unlike the organizations for hacks, cobs, riding horses and hunters, we allow and encourage stallions to compete in ridden classes because showing is a shop window. But safety and manners are paramount and if any exhibit – mare, stallion or gelding – looks to be a safety risk, it must be asked to leave the ring.

Standards in coloured showing classes have improved enormously. Ten years ago people were trotting round with pink girths and doing in-hand classes in wellies. Now the standards are as high as in any other showing class.

Our hardcore membership is made up of amateurs, but amateurs can and do have professional standards. We are getting increased interest from professionals, but I don't think that will or should deter anyone who really loves the coloured horse...and as our national show figures prove, there are plenty who do!

Lynda Lodge, chairman of the British Skewbald and Piebald Association

THE EXHIBITOR'S VIEW

I've wanted a top class coloured horse for a long time, but it had to be as good an example of its type as it was of a coloured horse and they aren't easy to find. I would never show anything just because it was coloured; I would have to be confident that I would like it as much as if it was plain bay.

My coloured horse, Triangulum, now sold, is as good an example of a cob as he is of a coloured horse, which is why he won his coloured class and was also well placed in his cob class at Wembley, in his first season of showing. If he wasn't, I wouldn't have been showing him.

Lynn Russell

Triangulum, a big winner in coloured and cob classes for Lynn Russell

28

Veterans

Classes for veteran horses are usually open to animals aged 15 or 16 and above – the lower limit depends on the show. Most are then sub-divided into categories, as it is difficult to compare, say, a 15-year-old with a 30-year-old. Judging is based on different considerations from straight showing classes and takes into account the horse's condition.

The Veteran Horse Society and Super Solvitax have launched a new series. Classes are divided into three age categories, which the VHS defines as pre-veterans, aged 15 to 20 years; veterans, aged 21 to 29 years and golden veterans, aged 30 years and over. Guidelines are laid down for judges to try and make classes as fair as possible, with 100 qualifying classes throughout the country leading to regional finals and an overall grand final at the Horse of the Year Show.

A JUDGE'S VIEW

Veteran classes are always going to be for amateur riders and much loved horses and ponies and over the past few years have become incredibly popular at local shows. They can be a nightmare to judge in that comparing a 17-year-old riding horse with a 32-year-old child's pony is far more difficult than sorting an ordinary class – but in general, the emphasis is on condition and soundness rather than conformation.

The good thing about them is that it makes more people realize that horses are not 'past it' at the age of 12. As we have become more knowledgeable about feeding and caring for older animals, so they are able to work happily for much longer. An elderly horse with a job is much happier than one who is bored and probably not getting as much attention and stimulus as he enjoyed in his earlier years – rather like elderly people.

3 RIDDEN SHOW AND NATIVE PONIES

Ridden and native ponies are responsible for starting many riders' lifelong interest in showing or in starting off their competitive careers. You only have to look at some of the big names who started their careers in the show ring – such as international dressage rider and trainer Jennie Loriston-Clarke and her sister, eventing star Jane Holderness-Roddam – to realize what a good grounding it can provide. The proviso is, of course, that parents realize that you can't necessarily go out and buy success, no matter how big your bank balance: any pony, no matter how successful it has been, will only continue in the same way if it is produced and ridden to the same high standards.

The big consideration with buying a ridden pony or a small native breed for a child to ride is that it must first and foremost be safe and suitable for its jockey. The larger categories presuppose a certain level of competence and you have to accept that with show ponies you are dealing with well-bred, quality animals who are likely to be sensitive and responsive rides. By the time a rider graduates to the 148cm (formerly 14.2hh) division, he or she will hopefully have had enough years of good teaching and practical experience to cope and make the most of such a pony – who, after all, are not police horses.

This means that taking on a pony to show, whether it be a show pony or a native, is a commitment for parents as well as children. It is essential that children receive good, regular tuition so that they learn to ride happily, safely and correctly in all circumstances and learn what is expected in the show ring. This applies to everything from performing an individual show to showing the appropriate behaviour if things go wrong or your pony is not placed as high as was expected or hoped.

It has to be said that this also applies to parents. Nothing is worse than the ultra-competitive parent who cannot accept it when things go wrong and starts haranguing the child as soon as he or she comes out of the ring.

AN EXPERT'S VIEW

Show ponies are not riding school animals, so you have to assume a certain level of competence on the part of the rider – certainly with the larger ones. Unfortunately, this isn't always the case: some people don't spend enough on tuition for their children, but instead spend their money on pretty browbands and posh rugs. One of the biggest mistakes is when parents buy novice ponies, thinking that their children will be able to school them. They won't: that's where the help and tuition comes in.

Royal Bronze, a 148cm show pony produced by Team Hollings and ridden by Anna Evans – winner of many championships and the first pony to win the supreme championship at the Royal International Horse Show (*Horse & Hound*)

Some parents are reluctant to buy a 'made' pony because they think that if it's been there and done it, the judges won't look at it any more. What they lose sight of is that a pony which knows its job can help a novice rider learn it and even more important, to enjoy showing. If they don't enjoy it, they'll simply get to the stage when they don't want to do it any more.

I can't stand it when riders come out of the ring and are immediately harangued all the way back to the stables. It's not the end of the world if something doesn't go quite according to plan – and if it is, you should get a life! Usually, they know when something went wrong and you can discuss it calmly and make sure it doesn't happen next time. I hate it when parents spend more than they can really afford on ponies because you know there's going to be too much pressure on the children.

Penny Hollings, producer and judge

If you look at a show catalogue, you will see a mind boggling array of classes for ponies, but in very basic terms they can be divided into three categories: the ridden or show pony, the show hunter pony and the working hunter pony.

The show pony is an elegant, free moving and well mannered animal with correct conformation. It must have all the conformation attributes that help to make it a good ride – a well set on head and neck, good shoulder and length of rein and good limbs. It must be comfortable and safe enough for its rider; for instance, a lead rein or first ridden pony should not be too broad or bouncy for a tiny rider.

Lead reins and first riddens are the smallest ponies and should not exceed 122cm (formerly 12hh). They are ridden by children who have not had their seventh birthday before 1 January in the current year and most shows specify that riders must be at least three years old. Even though they are under the control of a handler – who must be at least 16 years old – lead rein ponies must have impeccable manners. They are shown only in walk and trot: cantering is not allowed.

First ridden ponies are, as their name suggests, the next step up from lead rein ponies. The same rules on height and rider's age apply and they should be safe for a child to ride off the lead rein at all times. These ponies may be asked to canter in their individual shows, but are not cantered as a class.

The other ridden show pony categories, as laid down by the British Show Pony Society, are not exceeding 128cm (12.2hh); over 128cm but not exceeding 138cm (13.2hh) and over 138cm but not exceeding 148cm (14.2hh). There are age limits for the riders, which may vary depending on whether the pony is contending novice or open classes and which are specified by the relevant societies. The 128cm ponies may be galloped singly or in their individual shows, whilst the judge may ask the larger categories to gallop either

Wulfstan Stud's Clonbannin Cross, a successful working hunter pony (*Richard Weller-Poley*)

in their shows or in groups of not more than four ponies at a time.

Show hunter ponies should have the same qualities of conformation as the ridden show pony, but are more workmanlike and substantial. Their movement will be straight and true but not as elegant or extravagant. As the BSPS puts it, the judge looks for a hunter type pony with substance and good limbs which is fluent in all paces.

Again, they are divided into height categories with restrictions on the riders' ages: 122cm (12hh); over 122cm but not exceeding 133cm (13hh); over 133cm but not exceeding 143cm (14hh) and over 143cm but not exceeding 153cm (15hh). As you have probably guessed, if you are thinking of showing a pony you are going to spend a lot of time reading rule books!

Working hunter ponies must meet the same requirements on conformation, movement and type as their show hunter counterparts, but in addition must jump a course of 'natural' fences. Classes are judged in two phases, with marks awarded out of a possible total of 100. In the jumping phase, there are 50 possible marks for performance and 20 for style and manner whilst jumping. Knockdowns and refusals are penalized and a fall means automatic disqualification.

In the 'showing' phase, up to 20 marks can be awarded for conformation, type and freedom of action and up to 10 marks for manners. You do not need to be a mathematical genius to work out that a winning working hunter pony needs to be a real performer – however, the competition is so strong that you will be unlikely to do well unless its make, shape and movement are also of a good standard.

Finally, there are what can be the most confusing classes of all – the intermediate show riding types and intermediate show and working hunters up to 158 cm. These are restricted to riders not over 25 and were designed to act as a stepping stone between ponies and horses. Opinions seem to vary on whether or not they have succeeded, but they are proving popular and mean that a small riding horse or small hunter with a decent jump can be even more versatile, perhaps being competed by more than one member of the family.

Some judges accept that animals in intermediate classes can have a hint of 'pony' quality that would not be as acceptable in mainstream classes, though this would not necessarily be the case at the very highest level.

A JUDGE'S VIEW

There has definitely been a change in fashion over the past few years in the lead rein and first ridden classes, perhaps not always for the good. At one time these ponies would always either be little natives or have a fair amount of native blood, which gave them good temperaments. Now a lot of them are like little blood ponies – not that they can't be as well mannered and reliable as any other type, they can, but only if produced and handled correctly.

If you are a parent whose child wants to start off in showing and you're looking to do it fairly seriously, my advice would be to start off with a schoolmaster or mistress. Couple that with good instruction from someone who understands and gets on with children as well as understanding what is required for the show ring and your child will enjoy it.

It never fails to amaze me that seemingly sensible people can't accept that a safe, well-schooled pony is an investment for the future. A novice pony – no matter how nice and with how much potential – and a novice child is not a good combination.

The intermediates are a very mixed bunch. I'm not sure if the aim of the class, to bridge the gap between ponies and horses, was ever a realistic or even a necessary one, but there are certainly plenty of entries and I suppose it makes a horse more versatile. It also gives a 'home' to the well-made horse who perhaps does not otherwise fall into a definite category.

Natives

If anyone could bottle the success factor of Britain's native ponies they would make an instant fortune. Once thought of purely in terms of mounts for children, the large breeds in particular have shown that they can take on and often beat big horses in all disciplines – often defying stereotypes to do so. We now have all breeds, including the Fell, Dales and Highland 'hairies' doing endurance and affiliated dressage whilst others, especially the Connemara, are excelling in all spheres.

Although it is not a native breed, the Haflinger, which originates from Austria, is becoming increasingly popular. There is an annual breed show as well as show classes at many major shows, including Royal Windsor.

Add to that the incredible versatility of the part-bred, in particular the Connemara and Welsh Cob cross TB, and you have what in many people's eyes is the perfect package. A good native has presence, paces, good temperament and is cheaper to keep than, say, a TB or Anglo-Arab show hack. From the showing point of view, there is a wealth of classes available, from local level up to the mountain and moorland championship at Olympia.

Unless you subscribe to the school of thought (or snobbery) that a horse is not worth looking at or riding unless it is 16.2hh, you will also be pleasantly surprised at how easy it is for even a reasonably tall adult to ride a large native. A 14.2hh that follows its breed standard and is deep through the girth will take up the leg of any rider and a pony with a good front and length of rein will ride much bigger than its height.

Welsh Cobs and Dales ponies have no upper height limit and the 15 to 15.2hh Welsh Cobs are particularly popular. However, you will find that some competitions have a 14.2hh or 148cm height limit, though the time may come when that ruling is dropped. The big danger, as many knowledgeable breeders and judges have warned, is that in breeding for extra height we may end up with leggy animals that have longer than desirable cannon bones and are not deep enough through the girth.

Standards of production and riding in native classes have improved enormously over the past few years and inevitably, we are now seeing professional producers. However, there is still plenty of scope for the amateur owner/producer to win. Two things to keep in mind are that as well as being a good example of its breed, your pony must be well schooled and correctly turned out: rules on trimming vary between societies and judges are becoming much stricter. Natives are also slower to mature than TB types and a good one may not reach its prime until seven or older, so if you own a nice four-year-old you may have to be prepared to be patient.

The price of horses is dictated by supply and demand. As the demand for natives has increased, so have the prices of the top quality ones, in particular the Connemara. However, it is still possible to find a nice pony, particularly one of the other breeds, at a price below that of, say, a show hunter or hack.

A PRODUCER, JUDGE AND EXHIBITOR'S VIEW

Native ponies can do anything a horse can do and have so many advantages – for a start, they're usually much more intelligent! However, you have to make sure that this works for you, not against you. They are often a much better choice for a working owner, because they are more adaptable and easier to keep. The standard of showing has got much higher in recent years but it's still a very friendly world. People who show native ponies do so because they love them.

Although every pony is an individual, the breeds all have their own characteristics. A lot of Connemaras and Welsh Cobs tend to be quite dominant and, like all natives, have to be shown what the ground rules are. If you have a Welsh Cob you've got to have a bit of flair – you want to keep the flamboyance, but not let them drag you from pillar to post. In my experience, and I can only speak for the ones I've known, they can be quite unruly if they don't respect you. A lot of people will let their natives walk all over them, but that's a mistake. They're happier if they respect and trust you…and we keep them for our enjoyment, not the other way round!

New Forests are more laid back in general; you've only got to go the breed show and see all the stallions straight off the Forest. They're usually easier to break than Connemaras, but can be lazier, and tend not to take the initiative so much.

Highlands are also pretty laid back. They were originally bred to carry stags, not as riding ponies – and if you've got a 14-stone stag on your back, you don't go with your head up in the air! Having said that, I've ridden some that can go beautifully.

Exmoors are the purest of all the breeds. In my experience, they're looking for the easy life and you have to get them looking to you as their boss. Once they respect you, trust follows. That applies to all natives, but when I say you've got to get respect, I don't mean you should beat them up. I love watching them in the field: you can bet your life that the one who is boss in the field will be the one who is most awkward when you come to handle it.

The Dales and Fells I've had have probably had the nicest mixture of kindness and intelligence. High Heath Gunner, the Fell stallion, was nine when I broke him in and I won all sorts of things with him under saddle.

Julia Woods

A JUDGE'S VIEW

The show ring is vital for our native breeds, because it acts as a showcase for their qualities and a shop window for breeders. I feel very strongly that breeders, exhibitors and judges should all be fully aware of the breed society guidelines on conformation and realize that they have been laid down for a purpose: to protect these ponies' inherent soundness, hardiness and versatility.

It is inevitable that as ponies are now used much more for riding than for, say, carting stags or carrying loads of seaweed, the demand is for riding conformation: a sloping shoulder, good length of rein and all the other characteristics that make for a comfortable ride. But, and it is a very important but, we must not lose density of bone and strength of limb in a fashionable demand for taller ponies. For example, a 14hh Connemara who is well made, with relatively short legs and a deep girth, can take an adult rider just as easily as the 'up to height' 14.2hh/148cm animal which everyone now seems to be clamouring for.

Breed standards

As a guideline, these are some of the key points from breed societies, all of whom will provide full information.

Shetlands are usually ridden by children, though there have been occasions when adult judges have ridden them in open classes. A particularly memorable example was when Jennie Loriston-Clarke, a renowned judge as well as an international dressage rider, trainer and breeder, rode a Shetland exhibited before her in a mixed mountain and moorland class.

The other small breeds – Dartmoor, Exmoor, Welsh A, B and C – are usually, but not always, ridden by younger riders in the show ring. However, there are plenty that can and do carry adults and it must always be remembered that at one time many of them would have been used to carry farmers and shepherds on the hills. That in itself is a salutary reminder how important it is to preserve their soundness, toughness and density of bone.

Anyone unsure of any conformation terms can find them explained in chapter 4.

CONNEMARA

Characteristics – good temperament, hardiness and staying power. Intelligence and soundness, surefootedness and jumping ability, suitable for child and adult.
Height – 133cm to 148cm.
Colour – grey, black, bay, brown, dun, with occasional roan, chestnut, palomino and dark-eyed cream.
Type and conformation – compact, well-balanced riding type with depth, substance and good heart room, standing on short legs covering a lot of ground. Well-balanced pony head of medium length with good width between large, dark, kindly eyes. Pony ears, well-defined cheekbones, jaw relatively deep but not coarse. Head well set on to neck.

Chest not overloaded and neck not set too low. Well defined wither and good

Julia Woods on the
Connemara Kirtling
Mirabelle

sloping shoulder giving good length of rein. Deep body with strong back. Some length permissible but should be well ribbed up with strong loins.

Limbs should have good length and strength in forearm, well-defined knees and short cannons with flat bone measuring 18 to 21cm. Elbows should be free, pasterns of medium length, feet well-shaped of medium size, hard and level.

Hindquarters should be strong and muscular with some length, second thigh should be well developed and hocks strong and low set. Movement should be free and true without undue knee action, but active and covering the ground.

DALES
Characteristics – strong, sure-footed and intelligent, iron constitution and calm temperament.
Height – no official upper height limit but usually up to 14.2hh.
Colour – predominantly black, with some brown, grey and bay and, rarely, roan.
Type and conformation – renowned for their weight carrying abilities and ground-covering trot. Head should be neat, broad between the eyes but with no dish. Neck must be muscular and powerful with sufficient 'riding' length, set on to sloping shoulders.

The chest is broad and the body short coupled, with strong loins. Limbs should have well-defined tendons and the pony should have eight to nine inches of flat bone. The pasterns should be of a good length with very flexible joints and the hooves large, round and open at the heels, with well-developed frogs. Mane and tail hair and feather should be ample and straight.

Hindquarters are powerful and the hocks flat and well let down. Movement should be straight, true and powerful.

DARTMOOR

Characteristics – a good looking riding pony, sturdy yet with quality.

Height – not exceeding 12.2hh.

Colour – bay, black, brown, chestnut and roan. What the breed society terms as 'excessive white markings' are discouraged.

Type and conformation – head is small, quality and neat, with fine throat and jaws that show no sign of coarseness. A strong but not too heavy neck of medium length is set on to well laid back, sloping shoulders and mane and tail should be full and flowing.

The body is of medium length and well ribbed, with a good depth of girth giving plenty of heart room. Hindquarters and loins are strong and well muscled and neither level nor steeply sloping.

Forelegs should show a muscular forearm and fairly large, flat knee with short cannon bones and ample bone. Pasterns should be sloping but not too long and the feet should be sound, tough and well-shaped. Hindlegs should be well let down and movement should be low, straight and free-flowing, without exaggeration.

A well-schooled Dartmoor

Left: Native ponies should retain their breed characteristics, as shown by this Exmoor.

Right: Exmoor ponies in their natural habitat

EXMOOR

Characteristics – the oldest and purest of the native breeds and one which has unique characteristics: wide, prominent eyes surrounded by a rim of light hair, known as toad eyes, a coat of two layers which repels the worst weather and a 'mealy muzzle' with light coloured hair.

Height – up to 12.2hh for mares and 12.3hh for stallions and geldings.

Colour – bay, brown or dun, with black points. Mealy coloured hair on muzzle, round eyes and inside flanks; no white markings.

Type and conformation – sure footed and immensely strong. The head is large and well-shaped, not small and pretty. The pony should show a good length of rein with laid back shoulders and the chest must be deep and wide between and behind the forelegs. The back is level and broad.

Legs are clean and short and the action should be straight and smooth, without exaggeration.

FELL

Characteristics – hardy, with good pony characteristics, a lively and alert appearance and great bone.

40

Height – not exceeding 14hh (142.2cm)

Colour – black, brown, bay and grey, preferably with no white markings, though a star or a little white on the foot is allowed.

Type and conformation – Fell ponies have lots of personality, usually in the nicest way, and it must show! The head is small and well chiseled, with a broad forehead. Ears are small, well-formed and the there should be no sign of coarseness in the throat and jaw.

The neck should be in good proportion and give a good length of rein; it should be strong without being too heavy. Shoulders must be well laid back and sloping. The body is short-coupled, deep through the girth and round ribbed from shoulders to flank.

The Fell pony, shown here, and the Dales are similar in appearance. Fell ponies have an upper height limit of 14hh whereas there is no limit for the Dales. Both can carry heavy adults. (Clive Richardson)

Forelegs should be straight, with short cannon bones, at least eight inches of flat bone and a muscular forearm. Hindlegs should show good muscular thighs and second thighs and the hocks must be well let down.

The feet are of characteristic blue horn which is very strong and tough. They should be of good size, round, well-formed and open at the heels. A Fell pony should show a smart, true walk and a well-balanced trot with good knee and hock action. The hocks should come well under the body.

HIGHLAND

Characteristics – powerful, weight carrying pony with excellent temperament.

Height – 13hh to 14.2hh.

Colour – various shades of dun, grey, brown, occasionally bay and liver chestnut. Most ponies have a dorsal eel stripe and many have zebra markings on the forelegs. Apart from a small star, white markings are discouraged.

Type and conformation – head should be broad between the eyes and short between eyes and muzzle, with wide nostrils. The neck is strong and must not be too short and the throat clean, not fleshy.

Shoulders are well sloped and withers pronounced. The body is compact, the chest deep and ribs well-sprung. Legs should show flat, hard bone with clean joints and short cannon bones. Feather is silky and not over-heavy, ending in a prominent tuft at the fetlocks, and mane and tail hair should be long, silky and flowing, not coarse.

Highland ponies are enjoying a boom in popularity

New Forest ponies are popular because of their good temperament

NEW FOREST

Characteristics – strong, agile, willing pony with a good temperament who makes an ideal family all-rounder.

Height – no lower height limit, though ponies are seldom under 12hh, with an upper limit of 14.2hh.

Colour – any, except piebald, skewbald or spotted.

Type and conformation – New Forest ponies usually have good temperaments and are easy to train. They should be of a good riding type, with substance. You want to see an attractive 'pony' head, sloping shoulders, strong hindquarters and deep body. There should be plenty of bone and good hard, round feet and the action should be free, active and straight but not exaggerated.

SHETLAND

Characteristics – strong and robust with stamina and a general air of vitality.

Height – ponies are measured in inches, not hands and must not exceed 40 inches at three years or under and 42 inches at four years and over.

Colour – any known in horses, except spotted.

Type and conformation – the head should be small, in proportion and carried well; teeth and jaw must be correct and meet properly. The shoulder should be sloping, not upright, and the wither well defined. The body must be strong, with plenty of

A smart, active Shetland going well under saddle

heart room and strong, muscular loins, and the quarters broad and long.

Forelegs should have strong forearms, flat bone, short cannons and springy pasterns. Hindlegs should have muscular thighs and well-shaped hocks; when viewed from behind, the hindlegs should not be set too far apart and the hocks should not be turned in.

Feet must be tough, round and well-shaped and the pony should have straight, free action, using every joint and tracking up well.

WELSH SECTION A

Characteristics – the Section A, or Welsh Mountain Pony, is one of our prettiest breeds…but must also be sound, tough and intelligent. 'This is not a Barbie doll pony,' as one breeder puts it, 'it is a performer.'

Height – not exceeding 12hh.

Colour – any except piebald, skewbald or spotted.

Type and conformation – head should be small, with neat pointed ears, big, bold eyes and wide forehead. Jaw should be clean, tapering to a small muzzle and the silhouette may be dished, but never Roman (convex.) Neck should be of good length set on to sloping shoulders and clearly defined wither.

Limbs must be set square with good flat bone and round, dense hooves. The tail is set high and carried gaily and the action straight, quick and free, with hocks well flexed.

WELSH SECTION B

Characteristics, type and conformation – the Welsh Pony and Cob Society says that the Section B, or Welsh Pony, fits the general description of the Section A 'with greater emphasis being placed on riding pony qualities whilst still retaining the true Welsh quality with substance.'

Height – not exceeding 13.2hh

WELSH SECTION C

Characteristics, type and conformation – the WPCS explains that 'the Welsh Pony of Cob type is the stronger counterpart of the Welsh Pony, but with Cob blood.'

WELSH SECTION D

Characteristics – hardy, agile and with great powers of endurance, the Welsh Section D, or Welsh Cob, has been described as 'the best ride and drive animal in the world.' *Note: this is the only instance of a cob being a breed, which is why it is referred to with an upper case C. Otherwise, a cob is regarded as a type.*

Height – exceeding 13.2hh, with no upper height limit.

Colour – any except piebald, skewbald and spotted.

Broughton Last Express, ridden by Vicky Gibbons, shows the flamboyance of the Welsh Section D

Type and conformation – a quality head with pony character, featuring bold, prominent eyes, a broad forehead and neat ears. The body must be deep, on strong limbs with good joints and plenty of flat bone.

The action is vital: it must be straight, free and forceful, the knees should be bent and the whole foreleg extended from the shoulder and as far forward as possible in all paces, with the hocks well flexed, producing powerful leverage.

Of all the native pony societies, only that for the Shetland pony admits piebalds and skewbalds for registration. They claim that this is because they are protecting the 'purity' of the breed, but it is an issue that is causing some controversy, especially with the growing popularity of coloured horses and ponies. Their supporters point out that there has been evidence of coloured animals occurring naturally for many years. For instance, in the Welsh breeds these are known as 'crop-outs' and even when their lineage can be traced back through many generations of registered animals they are not allowed to be registered as pure-bred. They are starting to make their mark in coloured classes and other areas and it will be interesting to see if societies reconsider at some point.

4   CONFORMATION AND MOVEMENT

Ask any successful competitor to define the essential requirements for a show horse or pony, whether it be a heavyweight cob or an elegant hack, and good conformation and movement will always be top of the list. However, that's when it starts to get really interesting – because whilst it is possible to define the biomechanical necessities that make for a horse which is likely to stay sounder and give a more comfortable ride, it is impossible to find an animal which meets all of them. What you have to do, and what makes finding a good horse such a fascinating challenge, is learn to assess its plus and minus points and decide whether or not the overall picture comes out on the plus side.

Apollo when he arrived at Lynn Russell's yard as a naughty five-year-old with a reputation for being unrideable (Lynn Russell)

Apollo on his way
to one of many
championships,
including the Horse
of the Year Show
Cob of the Year

It is not just a case of being able to recognize that, say, a hypothetical horse is slightly short in the neck. You have to be able to look at the whole animal as well as its individual 'components', so you might decide that the length of the neck is perfectly acceptable because of the horse's type – he is a cob – and he is short coupled, with a workmanlike head that is much larger than a hack's or riding horse's but in proportion with the rest of him. In fact, if our hypothetical cob's head was grafted on to a longer neck, he would probably not be as well balanced, because he would be more likely to go on his forehand. Good conformation and good movement usually go together, because a horse who is correctly proportioned, with well-set on limbs, will move straight and have better natural balance. He will also, as long as he is correctly schooled, be a more comfortable ride than, say, the horse with an upright shoulder and pasterns and a 'sewing machine trot' – the sort who goes up and down rather than moving from the shoulder.

Occasionally you get a horse who looks the business but disappoints when he moves, or one which looks uninspiring and gives a pleasant surprise in action. You may also find a horse which should move well under saddle but doesn't, and is tight in the back, with a restricted stride. This can happen when a rider winches in the front end, via a double bridle or pelham, in a mistaken attempt to get the horse in a round outline, instead of working it so that it learns to use its hindlegs, move from behind and go in self carriage.

Conformation

The ability to judge conformation, often called having 'an eye for a horse' is something that can be learned – usually through dealing with and working many different horses and perhaps also learning from a few mistakes. The professionals who come out year after year with a new selection of lovely novices aren't just lucky and in many cases do not have limitless budgets. Instead, they have learned to spot the rough diamonds and know how work can transform a horse's shape as long as the basic skeletal structure is correct. If you are unconvinced, look at the 'before and after' pictures of some of show producer and dealer Lynn Russell's horses. Would you have spotted their potential in the rough, often in poor condition and only able to be judged standing in a muddy field, with hairy legs and manes halfway down their necks? And whilst it is nice to be able to see a horse walked and trotted up in hand on a level surface, could you assess its movement if this meant having to get the seller to chase it round that same muddy field, because the horse had not been taught to lead?

One of the best ways of learning how to assess conformation and that all-important quality of being true to type is to look at both ends of the winning line-ups at county shows. Although judges inevitably have individual preferences – because contrary to common belief, they are only human – the top horses should be good patterns. As judging is based on conformation and ride, you may sometimes feel that if you had been the judge, the places might have varied. Don't forget that you can see a lot more from inside the ring than from the outside and that a horse may have given a disappointing or 'green' ride, perhaps through its inexperience.

Look at the horses at the end of the line, too and ask yourself why they are there. Is the exhibitor trying to disguise conformation faults under a layer of fat? Does it perhaps have insufficient bone, weak hocks or a shoulder that is too straight?

In pony classes where the judge does not ride, the conformation and way of going should make you appreciate that a pony could not be anything other than a comfortable, balanced ride whilst at the same time retaining pony characteristics.

THE EXHIBITOR'S VIEW

I buy nearly all my horses from Ireland; I could count on the fingers of one hand the number I've bought in England over the past five years. I always buy young horses, so I'm not buying someone else's mistakes, and although they're usually fairly ignorant and often in poor condition, they haven't been spoiled. They certainly haven't been overfed, which means they're less likely to have joint problems.

It's quite funny when people come into the yard and say 'What's that thing?' then

Polaris, aged four years, a purebred Irish Draught who arrived with all parts in working order (Lynn Russell)

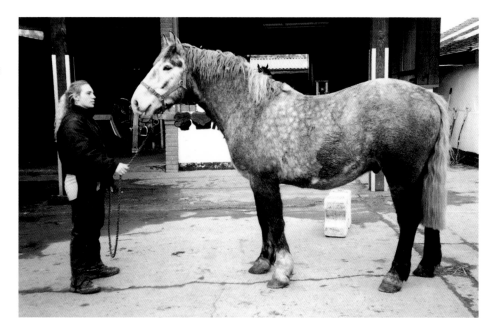

Polaris, later Horse of the Year Show Cob of the Year

see it a couple of months later and don't believe it's the same horse. I've got a lovely, lovely four-year-old lightweight cob who came over as a three-year-old. When he arrived it was like sitting on a rail with a pair of ears in your mouth, but correct feeding and work do make a dramatic difference as long as the basics are correct.

Another horse which arrived at the same time was a bit plain and a girl who worked for me at the time moaned that it was stiff as a board and not very nice to ride. I saw her on it in the field when I was on another horse and just had the feeling that it was a lot nicer than she thought. I got on it and within two minutes I knew I wasn't going to sell it, it was going to be a fabulous ride once it was schooled properly.

A lot of people assume I've got a special gift, but there's nothing magical about being able to spot potential. It's a mixture of experience and riding hundreds of different horses. Yes, I get a gut feeling that a horse is going to be a good one, but I don't have a crystal ball.

Lynn Russell

A JUDGE'S VIEW

When I'm assessing a class of ridden ponies, I look first and foremost at whether they are made to carry a rider, not whether they have a pretty head or flashy movement. Of course a show pony should be elegant in its appearance and way of going, but it must also be sound – there's no point in a fantastic daisy cutting trot if the pony has a deep body on spindly legs with insufficient bone.

Some exhibitors, not the most knowledgeable or successful ones, still seem to think that a pretty head is a top priority. It is, of course, part of the overall appearance, but you can do an awful lot to enhance appearance with the right bridle. Show hunter ponies, of course, are expected to be more workmanlike, whilst still retaining quality.

What do I want to see in a pony? Basically, a bold eye, well set on head and neck, good shoulder and a decent wither so the saddle stays where it's meant to be. The body should be deep enough for plenty of heart room and I like to see straight forelegs, clean joints and a strong second thigh.

Make and shape

To appreciate conformation, imagine you have a mature horse standing in front of you – or do just that with the real thing. It can be of any type, because the basic principles are the same whether you are looking at a show hack or a traditional coloured horse with lots of hair and feather.

The horse should stand square on level ground. When you look at him from the side, then ideally his body, without his head and neck, should fill a square. Ideally, you should see three matching sets of proportions: the length of the head should be the same as the length of the neck, the depth of the girth should match the length of the legs and the height should be the same as the horse's length from his shoulder to the end of his croup. Whilst you are taking in the overall picture, a few things might grab you straight away, for either the right or the wrong reasons. You might note that the horse has a lovely head with a bold eye, or that the lines of his body seem to flow into one another. Alternatively, your eye might be drawn to a lump on the inside of one foreleg or you might get the impression that he looks weak behind the saddle. First impressions are important, but don't fall in love with or write off a horse because of them.

HEAD, NECK AND SHOULDER

Just as you can't judge personality by a pretty or plain face, so you can't judge a horse solely from the appearance of its head. However, the proportions and type of head must fit in with the rest of the animal – though you can do an awful lot to enhance appearance by your choice of bridle. A large, open eye is attractive and a lot of people swear that the eyes give the key to a horse's character. This is not really fair, as a horse with small eyes is not necessarily mean or less genuine. Similarly, whilst showing the whites of the eyes is often said to indicate fear or wildness, this is not so unless accompanied by other warning signs such as tension or laid-back ears. Some horses simply show more white than others. Wall or blue eyes are frowned on in many types and breeds, though the British Skewbald and Piebald Association stipulates that its judges must not discriminate against horses with blue eyes. Such colouring does not affect the horse's eyesight, though some people find it unattractive. As with the shape of the head, it all comes down to the fact that if you have to see the horse looking over your stable door every morning, you need to like what you see!

The ears should be the same shape and size and set level and should also be in proportion to the rest of the head. As with eyes, it is all relative: you would not turn down an otherwise well-made horse because his ears were on the large or floppy side, but nor would you want a show hack that does a convincing impression of a donkey.

The conformation of the horse's mouth and jaw is important, as faulty jaw conformation can affect the way the horse eats. The upper and lower incisors should meet evenly and should not be badly overshot – often called parrot mouth – or undershot. Overshot means that the upper jaw is too long and undershot that it is too short.

The horse's teeth will tell you his age, though vets are becoming more and more wary

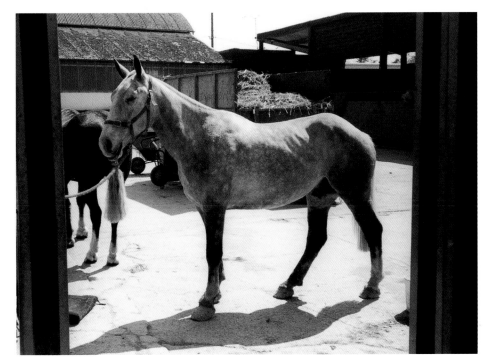

A potential show cob which – like so many – arrived in Lynn's yard from Ireland in poor condition. Three months' correct feeding and work have made a huge difference (Lynn Russell)

of committing themselves with regard to older horses during pre-purchase veterinary examinations – probably because we have become so much more litigation conscious. It is easy enough to age a horse up to seven years and many horses will have breeding documentation to confirm their age. Just be careful that the papers match the horse: this is something a vet should check during a pre-purchase examination, by matching up individual distinguishing marks such as whorls on the coat.

Check that the edges of the front incisors do not show excessive wear, which could mean that the horse is a crib biter. If the horse is a declared cribber, is in good condition and is excellent in all other respects, you may want to take the attitude that what he does in his spare time is his own concern. However, as with all stereotypic behaviour, it can affect his health and in 99 per cent of cases will lower his value.

Crib biting, where the horse holds on to and bites surfaces such as stable doors and windsucking, where he sucks in air at the same time, can predispose him to colic. There are collars which are said to prevent the habit, including one claimed to be of a particularly humane design, but any such behaviour is a sign of stress in a stabled animal. Unfortunately, some horses will also crib on field fencing and can cause a lot of damage. This behaviour can also cause a build-up of muscle on the underside of the neck, just where you don't want it.

Check the condition and conformation of the horse's mouth and tongue. Teeth with sharp edges will cause sores and ulcers on the insides of the cheeks and make the horse uncomfortable with his bit. These may only be visible to a vet or dentist using a gag, but if you run your fingers fairly firmly down the sides of the horse's face he may show a resentment to the pressure. Wolf teeth, small, shallow-rooted vestigial pre-molars that can be found in the upper and/or lower jaw, also interfere with the action of the bit. Both problems can be dealt with by a good horse vet or dentist.

Does the horse's tongue fit neatly into the lower jaw, or is it particularly thick? Thick tongues are not necessarily a problem as long as you take them into account when choosing a bit.

The way the horse's head is set on to its neck is very important, as is the connection between the base of the neck and the withers. There must be enough space behind the jawbone for the horse to flex easily, as if there is not enough room his breathing will be restricted and he may make a noise – an unforgivable fault in a show horse. You want to see a nice curve to the throat, not a sharp angle.

The neck should be of adequate length and ideally shaped so that the horse finds it easy to work in a good outline: he should be what is sometimes called 'born on the bit'. One of the worst faults is a ewe neck, which looks as if it has been put on upside down, but don't confuse poor skeletal structure with a horse in weak or poor condition. A horse with a true ewe neck is physically incapable of flexing properly and often goes with his head in the air and a hollow back. He is also naturally on his forehand, because his centre of gravity is shifted forwards. The horse with a neck that is too short and thick for his type will also find it difficult to flex correctly and may make a noise when asked to try and work in a round outline.

Another less often seen but faulty conformation point is the swan neck, which as its name suggests has a pronounced curve. At first glance this might seem to be acceptable, but the horse will not go correctly and again, will tend to hollow his back. Overtopped necks, with thick, heavy crests, are often down to overfeeding and are unacceptable – not least because overweight horses are prone to all sorts of health problems, including laminitis. The neck should flow on into the withers, not be set on too low. Low-set necks are often seen in Thoroughbreds bred for the Flat and in their job are not a conformation fault. The horse reaching for the finishing line will stretch out and lower his head and neck to overtake his rival, not gallop past the post perfectly on the bit. From the showing and dressage points of view, a low set neck is undesirable because it makes the rider's job harder. Correct feeding and work will help to build up muscles in the right place, but can't change the actual structure.

The withers themselves need to be well defined to help keep the saddle in the right place. In an ideal world they should not be too high, as this can cause problems with saddle fitting and also put the horse at a disadvantage when measured. A 15.2hh small hunter who is actually a 14.3hh horse with high withers will often look less impressive when standing in a line-up. There is an argument that when class rules stipulate lower and upper height limits, horses at the lower end of the scale should not be discriminated against. This is undoubtedly true, but unfortunately the good little'un will often lose out to the good big'un.

Cobs present the opposite problem and often have very little wither. When they are too fat, which sadly is still often the case, what little they have disappears into blubber. These horses are a saddle fitter's nightmare, as it is like trying to fit a saddle on a barrel. The angle of a horse's shoulder is vital and defines not only the way it moves but, to a certain extent, the ride it gives. The shoulder should have a good slope, as opposed to being upright; a more upright shoulder makes for strength and pulling power in a driving horse and is usually matched by upright pasterns, but results in a more up and down action, a shorter stride and a less comfortable ride. A horse with a good neck, withers and shoulder will also be easier to fit with a saddle and the saddle will stay in place. If the shoulder is upright, the saddle tends to slip forward and the rider's toes are uncomfortably close to the horse's elbows.

It took Lynn Russell's expert eye to see the potential in this Irish-bred youngster. He went on to become a successful lightweight show hunter (Lynn Russell)

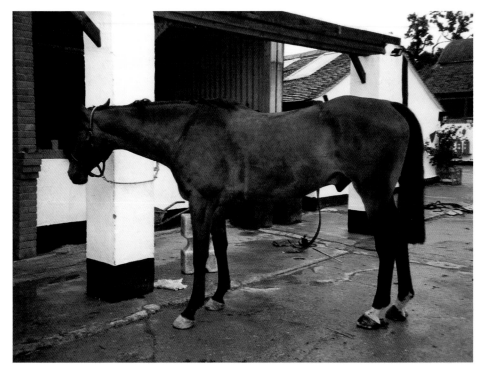

THE EXHIBITOR'S VIEW

Many people find it difficult to judge the conformation of a young, unfurnished animal, especially if it is in poor condition. It is equally easy for the untrained eye to miss faults that are hidden under layers of fat! The important thing to keep in mind is that a horse who is thin but made correctly will stay correct as he is fed and worked along the right lines. However, you cannot put right poor conformation.

Some things will always shine through even when a horse is thin – good movement; withers that are higher than the top of the quarters so that the horse is naturally built uphill; good limbs; a reasonable width to the chest.

Robert Oliver

THE BODY

Opinions vary on the ideal length of a horse's back, but the most sensible view is that the horse's frame should be reasonably compact, but certainly not too long or too short. A back that goes on forever – the sort that the old dealers used to describe as 'suitable for all the family: everyone can ride it at once' – can be weak, but it is all a question of degree. Mares are always slightly longer in the back than geldings because they need the extra space to carry a foal. As long as they are not weak in the loins, this is not a problem. If your interests lie in side-saddle, a slightly longer back can actually be an advantage because it makes it easier to fit a side-saddle.

At the other end of the scale, a back that is too short can cause just as many problems. If there is not enough room to fit a saddle, the horse will be taking weight on its loins. It is also more likely to forge and overreach (hit the back of the front foot with the front of the back one).

At one time, there was a school of thought that a short-backed horse was likely to be a better jumper. At lower levels, it may well be nippier and more adaptable, but at top level, riders now believe that a horse with a short back finds it harder to make the distance through combinations.

The back should be almost, though not quite, straight. A sway (dipped) back is weak and becomes more pronounced with age. The opposite, a roach (slightly convex) back is also weak. Both present problems in fitting a saddle and are not acceptable in a show horse. It is important for a horse to be deep enough through the girth, not only so that it will take the length of an adult rider's leg but so that there is enough room for the heart and lungs. The first consideration is borne out by the best native ponies, as a tall adult can look and feel absolutely fine on a good 14.2hh.

Look at the gap between the last rib and the line of the thigh. With a gelding or stallion, you should only be able to fit a handspan between the two. The distance can

Orbit, another top show cob who many people would not have looked at twice when he arrived at Lynn Russell's yard (Lynn Russell)

be a little greater with a mare, again because of the room she needs to carry a foal. If the gap is too large, the horse will find it harder to put its hindlegs underneath itself when it moves naturally and may also be more difficult to keep in good condition.

A herring-gutted horse, with a body profile like that of a greyhound or a super-fit TB that has just run a hard race, will also be difficult to keep in good condition. Apart from this, there will be a tendency for the saddle to slip back unless you use a breast-plate – which, of course, is not permitted in the show ring except in working hunter and cob classes.

The depth of girth is not just a question of aesthetics, as it also plays a part in the horse's weight carrying ability. The amount of bone (see next section) is vital when it comes to weight bearing, but a horse that has good bone and a deep girth will comfortably carry more weight than one with good bone but a shallow girth.

From the front and from the rear, the horse should stand foursquare. If the chest is too narrow, so that 'both legs come out of the same hole,' the horse will usually move badly. If it is too wide, he will probably have a rolling gait, but this is the lesser of the two evils. As always, assessment must be made according to the horse's type: a cob will be broader through the chest than a hack, though both may be correct as individuals. Any equine athlete, including the show horse, should look as if the front matches the back. You therefore want to see a good back end to match a good front one and not just for reasons of aesthetics. The horse's 'engine' is sited in his hindquarters and though correct feeding and work will enable you to build up his muscles, the underlying structure must be sound.

Cobs in particular have naturally powerful back ends. This, coupled with the fact that they do not mature physically until they are six or seven years old, means that you have to accept that many four and sometimes five-year-olds go through stages where the back end is often higher than the front. This means that they may find it difficult to balance themselves, as they are temporarily downhill, and their schooling must be planned to take this into account.

You hope to see a broad, fairly flat croup; a goose rump with a pronounced bump at the top is sometimes said to be a sign of natural jumping ability, but it can also be a sign of weakness. Ideally, the tail should be set on neither too high nor too low. A well-bred horse's tail will have a thinner dock and finer hair than a cob's, whilst a naturally high tail carriage is often a sign of Arab blood.

LIMBS AND FEET
Just as a building can only be as secure as its foundations, so a horse can only be as sound as its limbs and feet. Even a TB small hack will weigh around 500kg, whilst a heavyweight hunter will be 600kg or more. When you look at the strain a horse puts

on its legs when galloping or jumping, it is easy to understand why the old dealers liked a horse with a pretty head to appeal to susceptible customers, but started their own assessment from the ground up!

Your first impression should be that the horse's limbs match his body: in particular, that you do not have a powerful, chunky body set on spindly legs. When you look at him square on from the front, you should be able to draw two imaginary, parallel lines from the points of the shoulders that bisect the forelegs and make right angles with the ground. The measurement between the centres of his hooves should be the same as that between the points of his shoulders. If it is greater, he is base wide and will be taking extra strain on the inside of the forelegs and feet. If it is smaller, he is base narrow and the strain will be taken on the outsides of the limbs and feet.

The forearm – the part of the foreleg coming out of the shoulder – should be broad and long, but the cannon bone below the knee should be short. This gives not only the best proportions for bearing weight and taking strain, but a sufficiently long, comfortable stride.

The knees should be wide, flat and at the same height and you should avoid a horse who is markedly back or over at the knee. Back at the knee means there is a concave outline between the bottom of the knee and the fetlock, whilst over at the knee means this outline is convex. The other common fault is when a horse has a noticeable indentation at the back of the knee, known as 'tied at the knee'. Any marked variation from the ideal puts some strain on the tendon.

Splints, bony growths on the insides of the foreleg, are a drawback in the show horse. Many judges will forgive a small splint as long as it is not in a position that means it will interfere with the action of the knee joint, but – as with any blemish – if the final judging comes down to two horses of equal merit and one has a splint, the horse with clean limbs will always come out on top. Splints usually form as a result of a strain or a blow and can be caused by something as simple as a young horse galloping in the field or getting kicked. If a youngster you have bought or bred develops one, it is worth getting veterinary advice as in some cases, they can be reduced. Some horses go lame whilst they are forming but once the splint has hardened, it will rarely cause any problems unless near a joint.

All show horses need to be capable of carrying a rider of the appropriate weight. One of the major factors in deciding this is the amount of bone, which is measured round the widest part of the cannon bone, just below the knee. It is all part of the overall conformation picture – for instance, a horse with plenty of bone but long cannon bones will probably carry less weight than the animal with adequate bone and shorter cannons – but the accepted guidelines are that a lightweight hunter should have about eight and a half inches of bone, a middleweight about nine inches and a heavyweight nine to nine and a half inches.

A lightweight cob should have at least eight and a half inches and a heavyweight nine inches or more. This is one area where the horse world refuses to go metric! A hack will usually have less bone than any of the other show horse categories, but must never be light of bone. This is a particularly contentious area, as the champion hacks of the late fifties had more bone and substance than those of today and some experts believe that this 'fining down' is detrimental to soundness.

As with all joints, the fetlocks should look to be a matching pair. The commonest blemishes in this area are windgalls, enlargements of fluid sacs around the pastern or fetlock joints, but these are not usually a problem unless they are very noticeable. Pasterns should have sufficient length and slope to absorb concussion as the horse moves. If they are too long, it puts strain on tendons and ligaments and if too short, every step will jar; hind pasterns are naturally slightly shorter than front ones. The slope of the pasterns should match the slope of the shoulder.

The proportions of the hindlegs are equally important. The second thigh, or gaskin, should be well defined, but can be built up dramatically through correct work if the basic structure is right. Hocks should be a matching pair: wide, deep and not too straight. If you stand behind the horse, you should be able to visualize perpendicular lines dropping from the points of the buttocks to bisect the hocks, cannon bones and heels.

Avoid a horse with sickle hocks, where the leg comes in front of a perpendicular line drawn from the point of the hock to the ground, because these are a sign of weakness. Cow hocks, which turn inwards, are not usually such a problem in terms of soundness unless the defect is pronounced but are still undesirable.

Curbs, swellings on the back of the hindleg just below the hock, are one of the biggest conformational sins in the show ring. They can be 'true' or 'false' – a false curb will disappear when you pick up a hindleg whilst a true one will remain – but you don't want to see either.

Other hindleg blemishes to watch out for are bog spavins, thoroughpins and capped hocks. The first means that the natural depression on the front of the hock is filled and such a horse is often described as having 'boggy hocks.' A bone spavin is much more serious from the soundness point of view but is often only detected by X-ray, perhaps because the horse fails a hindleg flexion test during a pre-purchase veterinary examination. Capped hocks are a blemish, not an unsoundness, but will be a big black mark against a show horse. This term describes fluid-filled enlargements on the point on one or both hocks, usually caused by the horse kicking the walls or scraping his hocks on a concrete floor – so the moral of this story is that you should never stint on the amount of bedding used. Thoroughpins are swellings above the hock joint near the Achilles tendon. They will not make a horse lame but again, are an extra you can do without.

If your 'guinea pig' show horse has passed scrutiny so far, there is one vital test he must pass: he must have good feet. Good feeding and farriery can work wonders with the horse who is lacking in nutrients and general care, but the basics have got to be right. This means that a horse should have two matching pairs of feet; you don't want to see that one front or hind foot is a different size or shape from its partner. Look from behind as well as in front and feel round the coronet to check that there are no lumps or ridges. The angle of the foot should follow the angle of the pastern, not form a broken axis – though faulty trimming can sometimes be to blame. The feet should be open, not boxy, and in proportion to the size of the horse. You don't want to see pony feet on a big hunter or soup plates on a hack.

Flat feet predispose a horse to bruising and a fungal infection called thrush. A good foot will have a moderately concave sole, well-defined frogs and open heels. Weak, splitting hooves can be a real problem, as the horn crumbles around the nailholes, resulting in frequently lost shoes. There are now several nutritional supplements formulated to improve the rate and quality of horn growth and some undoubtedly work well in some horses. However, as one leading orthopaedic vet puts it: you can supply the nutrients your horse might be lacking, but you can't guarantee that he will be able to absorb them.

A JUDGE'S VIEW

When I stand in the centre of the ring and my class comes in and starts to walk round, there are usually two or three animals which make an instant impression – for either the right or the wrong reasons! Perhaps there is a horse which immediately 'fills the eye' because it is so symmetrical and pleasing in its proportions, or one which has a stilted, shuffling walk.

There will be times when you see a horse stripped and find that it is not as nice as you thought it was when you saw it under saddle, but you still have to keep in mind the overall picture. Different people have different likes and dislikes; I can forgive a small splint if the horse has an otherwise good foreleg, but I know some judges who can't bear them. I'm not bothered by acquired blemishes, such as scars, in hunters as I take the view that they may hopefully be honourable badges of work. I would note their presence in a hack or riding horse, especially in a hack where you're looking for elegant perfection, but would not let them put me off placing an otherwise nice horse. It's the old thing that if in the final crunch it came to two horses and the only thing tipping the balance was that one had a scar, then it would have to be the deciding factor.

One thing that I can't forgive is a curb and I know I'm not alone. In fact, I don't know a single judge who would not penalize a hindleg with a curb. It surprises me the amount of exhibitors who don't know what one is – whilst I would never point out a defect, if someone asks me for advice after the class I am happy to give my opinion and on several occasions, riders have not realized what it is or its significance.

Movement

The way a horse moves depends, to a great extent, on its conformation. Occasionally you get a well-made horse whose movement disappoints, or, more rarely, an ordinary looking animal with spectacular movement.

A sloping shoulder and pastern and long forearm is the basis of a good stride with not too much knee action, whilst a straight shoulder will give the up and down trot of the draught horse. If the limb is straight and the horse is neither base wide, base narrow or wide behind, he will move straight.

Hunters, cobs and riding horses should show a good gallop

The powerful, straight movement of a show hunter – Veronica Dawes on the Rawdings' Reaction

Hacks must also move straight, but it is important that their movement is as elegant as their appearance. Kate Moore on Poetic Justice

Obviously the ideal in any show horse is straight movement with good natural rhythm. You may get away at some levels with one that turns a front toe slightly, provided everything else is spot on, but a horse which dishes to the extent that it swings out a leg from the shoulder will be heavily penalized – not so much because it is unattractive, but because it puts extra strain on the skeletal and muscular systems and is therefore a weakness.

The horse who brushes – strikes one leg with the hoof of its opposite pair – is obviously more likely to injure itself. Plaiting, where one front foot comes across and in front of the other, again puts strain on the limbs…and as the horse is likely to trip itself up at speed, you wouldn't want to gallop one which moved like this.

There are subtle differences in ideal movement according to the horse's type. At one end of the spectrum is the hack, which should move in a low, elegant fashion, pointing his toe without any knee action: what is often termed a 'daisy cutter'. A hunter or cob will be much more workmanlike, but whilst a cob will usually show a slightly rounded knee action, it should not be obvious or exaggerated. A riding horse's movement will be smooth, straight but still workmanlike, tending more towards that of the hunter than the hack.

THE EXHIBITOR'S VIEW

When I'm assessing the way a horse moves, I want to see him led out on a slack rope so I see his natural movement – provided he's been taught to lead! If you're looking at something unhandled, in the field, it's sometimes a case of getting the seller to chase it up and relying on experience.

If it's a horse I'm thinking of buying, I'm looking for soundness as well as the quality of the movement, so I like to see it go from the front, the back and from both sides. I'll start by watching the horse walk away from and then back towards me and if I see a free, generous walk stride I know we've started on a good note. A horse that can walk can gallop, as racehorse trainers will tell you – that's how they choose yearlings, on the quality of the walk.

Ideally the horse will overtrack: in other words, the imprints of the hindfeet will overtrack those of the forefeet. The length of stride and degree of overtracking depends to some extent on the type of horse. Cobs tend to be more short striding than hunters or riding horses and the walk is not their naturally best pace; if you get a cob with a good walk, it's a real bonus.

The trot is the pace that shows up any unsoundness or movement defects. If an otherwise lovely horse turns a toe or is a bit close behind, you might make an exception if you don't want to show at top level. If you're aiming for the cream of the county circuit and above, you've got to have straightness and rhythm.

There are ways of improving a horse's paces, but one that is born with the right attributes is always the best choice.

Lynn Russell

A JUDGES' VIEW

I always like to see a horse with a good walk. It catches my eye on first impressions and if I'm torn between two horses, the final walk round will often make up my mind. A lot of riders let their horses down at this pace, either by slopping along or winching in the horse's head and restricting the movement.

I like to see a canter and trot that are both rhythmical, forward but unhurried. A lot of people trot too fast and canter too slow. There's also an art to running horses up in-hand that many amateurs seem not to appreciate. They should watch the professionals do it and see how they keep their horses balanced, not suddenly firing them into trot on a turn. Everyone has the idea that show ponies should move with an extravagant trot and certainly their movement should be elegant, straight and light with minimal knee action. But whilst older children can ride bigger movement, you certainly do not want a big moving lead rein or first ridden, nor do you want one with a bouncy stride. These ponies are meant to be safe conveyances for small children, who don't have the length of leg or security of seat to be much more than passengers – so the pony should be a straight, neat mover who will help its little rider feel comfortable and confident.

Show hunter and working hunter ponies are by definition more workmanlike in type and you wouldn't want to see them flicking their toes. Their movement should, of course, be dead straight, but a slight roundness of action is perfectly acceptable as long as the pony moves from the shoulder and not in an up and down way. In fact, with the workers, a slight roundness and lift to the stride is often a sign that the pony will be a good jumper.

5 THE QUIRKY BITS

You might be tempted to think that finding a horse with good conformation and movement is all you need to succeed in the show ring. Wrong! As with all things to do with horses, there is a huge collection of pieces to make up the final jigsaw, especially if you have to combine keeping your horse with holding down a job and/or family commitments. It is impossible to lay down hard and fast rules that will suit every set of circumstances, but there are aspects that everyone should consider – the quirky bits that you ignore at your peril.

Temperament, presence and gender

No matter what type of horse or pony you are showing, there is one final piece of conformation that is absolutely vital – the bit between the ears. A good temperament can mean the difference between enjoyment and frustration, especially for the amateur owner rider. A professional rider may have the skill, knowledge and time to cope with a difficult horse, but if your horse is part of your life and you ride for enjoyment the scenario may be different.

Most of us with family and/or work commitments have limited time and cannot, for instance, work a horse three times a day for very short periods if that is what is needed to get the best out of it. Similarly, it takes an exceptionally capable rider to cope with a horse who is particularly nervous or excitable. No matter how good looking the horse is, it isn't going to give you pleasure or success if it consistently bolts, bucks or rears in the ring with you.

A good temperament does not necessarily mean a horse who is affectionate in the stable or who could have an alternative career as a police horse. It means that if you get everything right in terms of feeding, management, schooling and presentation, you will be able to ask the right questions and get the right answers.

The best show horses are bright, even cheeky, but willing. They are natural show-offs, with an air about them of 'look at me'. This star quality is all part of a good temperament, but is also defined as presence, a charisma that can be seen in all the best show animals, whether they be cobs or Connemara ponies.

Finally, there is the question of gender. If you want to light the fuse of a fierce and long-running debate, ask any rider about the various merits and drawbacks of mares and geldings. Everyone agrees that geldings are generally more easy going, but whilst some people are prepared to treat all horses as individuals, others will not consider buying a mare because they believe they are unpredictable in general and especially when in season. When it comes to making a decision on this subject, you are on your own. One advantage of owning a successful mare is that if or when her ridden career comes to an end, she has a second job as brood mare. On the whole, geldings are more easy going…but remember the old saying that all generalizations are false, including this one!

THE EXHIBITOR'S VIEW

I know a lot of people are prejudiced against mares and will only have geldings, but I've always loved a good mare. When you get a really good one, she can be hard to beat because she often has a natural presence. In one way, a mare is like a stallion in that nothing has been taken away!

There is a lot of truth in the old saying that you tell a gelding, ask a mare and discuss it with a stallion. You have to make a mare want to work with you, not say 'You will do this.' That applies to all horses, of course, but especially towards a mare.

We've had some mares on our yard that have been quite complex characters, but once they know you and trust you they will often do their best. There is also the bonus that a successful mare will hopefully be equally successful as a broodmare when her career in the ring is over.

Kate Moore

Stereotypic behaviour/stable vices

One of the most unfair aspects of keeping horses is the way we change their lifestyles dramatically from the way nature intended and then label them as neurotic when they cannot cope with it. Horses are born to roam over large areas, not to stand in confined spaces, and though many of them are perfectly happy being stabled part of the time, others are not. The ones who are unhappy at being stabled often develop what are commonly called stable vices. Researchers now give these a different and fairer label: stereotypic behaviour. After all, the horse cannot help his behaviour and it is now thought that it gives him some relief from mental stress by creating endorphins, chemical substances generated naturally in the body which produce a natural 'high.'

One school of thought now preaches that we should think of stables as prisons and that every horse is happiest when turned out 24 hours a day. A lot of horses have not read that particular manifesto and whilst they enjoy their freedom in the field, are content to be stabled for part of the time and stand at the gate almost asking to come in when the weather is bad.

However, if you are buying a show horse and find that the only 'but' is a form of stereotypic behaviour, you have to decide if the pros outweigh the con. There are three patterns known as declarable vices: in other words, the seller should disclose them. These are the previously mentioned crib biting and windsucking, plus weaving. Weaving, where the horse sways his head from side to side over the stable door, varies in its intensity and frequency. In mild cases, the horse will move his head from side to side over the stable door and may only do it in anticipation of feed arriving. In bad ones, he will shift his weight from one foreleg to the other, obviously putting strain on his limbs. You can try and minimize it by installing a V-shaped anti-weaving grid on the stable door, but the best solution is to keep him outdoors as much as possible.

Apart from the risks of health problems such as colic or limb strain, a horse who shows this sort of behaviour may be difficult to keep weight on. Unless he is so amazingly stunning in all other respects that no one could turn down the chance of owning him, he will also be worth less than if he was 'viceless' – good news, perhaps, if you are buying him but not so good if you ever have to sell him.

THE EXHIBITOR'S VIEW

From a dealing point of view, I'd be reluctant to take a horse with stable vices because they're so much harder to sell. If I found a horse who was absolutely stunning and intended to show him myself, I might accept and cope with a weaver because I have the facilities to keep him happy.

In my experience, horses who weave in a normal stable show no signs of doing so when in a stall, where they have neighbours on either side that they can see and touch. We also have a large, open-fronted barn where we can keep two compatible horses together and this also makes a weaver much happier.

Lynn Russell

Age

Another aspect you have to think about is whether you want a young horse who is ready to start his showing career, a more mature one who perhaps has some ring experience or an old hand who will act as a schoolmaster. Some people may want to buy a yearling, two or three-year-old and show it in hand before it starts a career under saddle, but this can be a difficult area.

Although the occasional in-hand outing can give a youngster good experience, many experienced producers feel that yearlings are better off being left in a field to grow and mature than subjected to the pressures of showing. There is also the point that unless the exhibitor is skilful and careful, a young horse's mouth may be spoilt – particularly if it is a three-year-old tacked up in a double bridle, as is sometimes seen.

The number of in-hand stars who go on to become successful ridden show horses is frighteningly low. It may be simply that the perfect duckling becomes an ugly swan, but it may also be that the exhibitor who gets a young horse too fat in the mistaken belief that he or she is producing it in 'show condition' puts too much weight on immature limbs, resulting in unsoundness.

Another problem is that the youngster who is over shown may become so fed up with the whole business that it loses its presence and sparkle.

THE BREEDER AND EXHIBITOR'S VIEW

It can be an advantage if a pony has been shown in-hand a few times in that it gets them used to travelling and to all the sights and sounds – loudspeakers, ice cream vans and all the other hazards you have to cope with. But it's even more important not to overshow them, because they either switch off or get naughty.

I don't think a lot of people realize how stressful it can be for a youngster at a show. They don't have long concentration spans when they're babies and you have to be careful it doesn't all get to be too much for them. I never show mine more than three times a year in-hand. Ideally, they go out twice as a yearling, twice at two and twice at three. Then they're not fazed by it by the time they get to their first ridden shows, they've travelled and stood on the box and heard all the loudspeakers.

Julia Woods

Most professionals prefer to buy their own horses as three or four-year-olds and do the initial work at home before starting them off in the ring as novices. This has two advantages: they are not having to sort out someone else's problems and the horse is a 'fresh face' to the judges.

Many amateur riders also prefer to buy an unshown or lightly shown four or five-year-old and again, there can be very good reasons for doing so. Whilst a young, inexperienced horse of the right stamp will always command a good price, it will not usually be as expensive as a five to nine-year-old that has a good showing record and knows its job. It is also very rewarding to know that any successes you achieve are down to your own hard work.

However, if you are going to bring on a young horse you must be a decent rider and have the facilities and – in most cases – help at hand. There are riders who have produced horses by schooling on hacks and in the corner of a field, but they are the minority. A young horse also demands time and commitment and unless you are sure that you will be able to find both at the end of a busy working day, you might run into problems. The most expensive horse to buy initially is the made show horse between five and eight who has proved that he can do well and still has the chance to do better. However, there is no such thing as a rosette machine on four legs. No matter how nice the horse, it still has to be produced and ridden correctly and a horse's schooling can go backwards just as fast as it can go forwards.

You sometimes hear of people buying horses from well-known competitors only to find that instead of heading the line-ups, as they expected, they can only pick up lower placings. The cry then is 'It's because judges look at the faces on top' – but the real story is that the previous face on top knew how to get that horse looking and going at its absolute best and the new owner does not have the same skill.

What you may find, if you want a horse that will do well at a reasonable level but are not determined to win at Wembley, is that a professional exhibitor may bring out a young horse and decide during or after its first season that it probably won't make the very top. As this is their sole objective, they will then sell the horse to make room for the latest potential star. This sort of horse will not come cheap, but can be a great investment. You still have the scope to progress and you know that if you do everything right, the horse has the basic qualities to do well at, say, agricultural and county level. There have even been cases where a professional rider has sold a horse only to be beaten by it, perhaps because the horse has thrived in a one to one relationship or matured beyond expectations. Older horses have a lot to offer if they have the temperament to act as schoolmasters to novice exhibitors, but again, there are pros and cons to consider. Once a horse gets to nine or ten, he is usually at the peak of his career and if he hasn't won major honours by then, realistically it is unlikely that he is going to do so. It is also a fact of life that the older a horse gets, the more likely he is to develop soundness problems: for instance, like us, horses are more prone to stiffness and arthritis as they age.

A horse in his early teens will be cheaper than a younger animal of the same quality, but you also have to ask yourself what you expect from him. He will give you confidence in the ring, but where do you go from there? Showing a horse who has done well at top level in local shows is, quite frankly, pot hunting. Also, an older horse is not necessarily an angel on four legs. The sort who says 'I'll do it properly if you do it properly' is wonderful for teaching you to get it right, but the one who has become bored with showing and knows all the tricks – tanking off in the gallop or napping – is no fun.

Many caring owners of top class horses who reach the end of their careers are reluctant to sell them into showing homes, often for the right reasons. They don't want to see them going down and down the line and often want to see them go out at the top and enjoy a new lifestyle. Some switch careers to dressage and there have been several top class working hunters who have gone into show jumping; others become hunters or much-loved pleasure horses. The increasing popularity of veteran classes may mean that more horses carry on showing in this sphere, particularly with the Veteran Horse Society/Super Solvitax series of competitions.

Different considerations perhaps apply to buying ponies – almost certainly so if you are looking for a partner for a novice child. The pony with experience, who will not be phased by all the sights and sounds of the show ring and can be guaranteed to stay calm in trying circumstances, will give a child confidence and enjoyment. The young, novice pony needs the rider who will give him confidence, which is a different ballgame altogether.

Height

If you are buying a horse or pony to show in a category which requires a height certificate, then it is vital to make sure that it will measure in. Height certificates need to be obtained annually until the age of seven; as this book was going to print the Joint Measurement Board – the organization which controls the scheme and to which organizations such as the British Show Pony Society and British Show Hack, Cob and Riding Horse Association belong – announced that all championship winners at the Horse of the Year Show, even those with life certificates, would have to be re-measured.

If the animal you are thinking of buying is under seven years of age and is already well up to height, you therefore have to decide whether or not to take the risk that it will stay within the height limits. Cobs and mountain and moorland ponies in particular are usually not fully mature until they are at least seven, so the nice five-year-old that is still a bit higher behind than in front could be a gamble even if it does hold an annual height certificate.

Nor is it a case of being able to try again if your first attempt at getting a horse measured fails. If you can measure your horse or pony at home but are not sure whether you have the skill or the confidence to do the same in strange surroundings, it might be worth asking a professional to do the job for you. You will have to pay a fee, especially if you send your horse or pony in advance so it can be taught to stand correctly and quietly, but as the difference between a 148cm champion show pony and a 148.1cm hard luck story can be thousands of pounds and a lot of disappointment, it can be worth it.

It is not that professionals cheat, even though there are always cases where another hair on the withers would have pushed a horse over the limit, but rather that they know how to prepare animals. Also, a professional showing yard will inevitably have a regular farrier who knows exactly how to trim an up-to-height animal's feet to give it every chance, without going too far.

Breed it or buy it?

The saying that 'Fools breed horses for wise men to ride' may seem to have a lot of truth in it when many breeders find it hard to recoup the costs incurred in raising a youngster, let alone make a profit. But – fortunately for the rest of us – there are some people who are prepared to take the risk and who get enormous pleasure in trying to breed horses with star potential.

Most agree that the best approach is to use only mares with good conformation, movement and temperament and to send them to stallions with the same qualities. You then stand the best chance of breeding a potential equine athlete who, if he does not fulfil the requirements of the show ring, has a future in another sphere. The problem can be that not only are you trying to breed a good horse, you are trying to breed a good horse of a particular type.

In the case of hunters, hacks and riding horses, this aim is perhaps not so difficult to achieve. But with other categories, such as small hunters, cobs and coloured horses, there is an element of luck. It is often said, for instance, that the best cobs are accidents of birth and certainly the majority have unknown origins. Notable exceptions include Lynn Russell's Polaris, a phenomenally successful heavyweight cob who is actually a pure-bred Irish Draught by the ID stallion Silver Jasper. However, another of Lynn's former stars from a different breeder had a full brother who only grew to 14hh.

Buying from a breeder can be ideal if you are in the market for a youngster, especially if you are able and prepared to back it and bring it on. You can often see at least the dam, if not the sire, and know its full history.

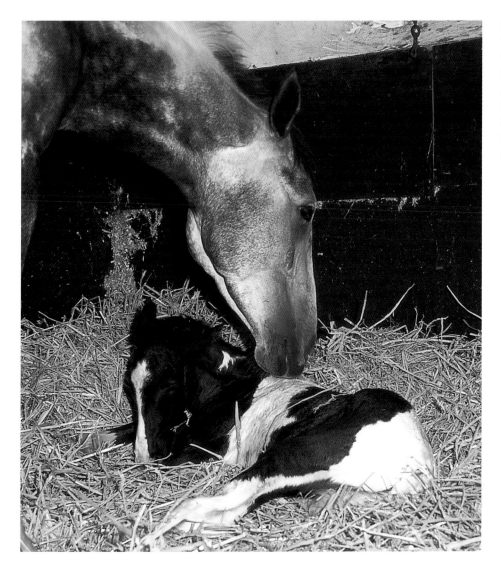

Breed it or buy it? The newborn Wulfstan Andante, by Wulfstan Amadeus out of Rainbow Dancer, by Loch Pearl, should make a top class coloured show horse

SOME BREEDERS' AND EXHIBITORS' VIEW

There is something special about being successful on a homebred horse. It was a great thrill for us to do so well with Ambershire Fort George, and I hope that my small hack Treverva Verity's daughter will do as well as her mother. But no matter how careful you are, there is always an element of luck – you hope for a sound, well-made youngster first and that it will do well in the show ring second. If it is not a show horse, perhaps because it does not fit into a height category, then at least it has the potential to go on in another sphere.

Kate Moore

Kate Moore with the
homebred small
riding horse,
Ambershire Fort
George

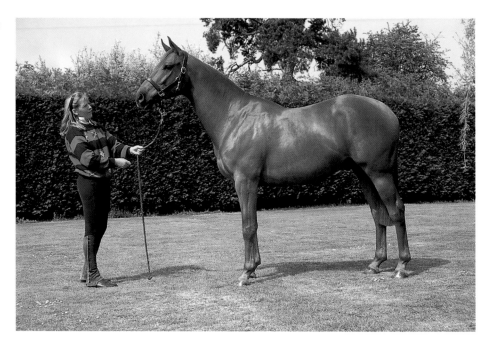

Over the years we have bred some very good horses, perhaps the best of which was
Realistic. Sadly, he died as a five-year-old from inoperable colic and we never got to
see how good he could have been. I think in general that top class horses are so hard
to find, you're best to buy one if you're lucky enough to find it at the right price and
hope that by breeding from correct stock, you get correct offspring.

Sue Rawding

Good show horses are made, not bred. It's not enough to breed a good looking,
good moving horse – it has to be correctly produced and ridden. However, when a
horse's breeding is known, as with Polaris, who is a pure-bred Irish Draught by Silver
Jasper, I will always give credit to the breeder when filling in entry forms for
catalogue details.

Lynn Russell

Where to buy

There are four main ways to buy a potential show horse – from its breeder, from a
private seller, from a dealer or at auction. There are also a few specialist agencies which
link sellers and buyers of particular types, such as coloured horses; if you are looking
for a native pony, the breed societies produce sales lists in which breeders and
members advertise animals for sale. Finding horses for sale is easier than ever, thanks

to the number of equestrian magazines carrying advertisements and the various websites. However, finding the right horse is not so simple!

Although it might sound obvious, many people forget that buying a horse is a lot more complicated than buying a car, simply because it is an animal with a mind of its own whose behaviour and way of going depends on how it is treated, looked after and ridden. Every horse is an individual and one which is happy on a busy yard with plenty to watch might be less happy in quiet surroundings – and, of course, vice versa. So whilst you can do your best and consumer law should give you protection against downright dishonesty, the traditional bywords Caveat emptor – 'Let the buyer beware' – always apply and should be kept in mind.

The law relating to the buying and selling of horses is complex. However, it is fair to say that although the Sale of Goods Act 1979 covers all transactions, it offers more protection to the vendor if the horse was purchased from a dealer, someone who sells as a business, than from a private seller. That in itself is farther complicated by the fact that someone who sells horses in a limited capacity, perhaps a breeder who produces youngstock to sell, may be considered to be selling as business. Then there are the people who insist that they are not dealers but nevertheless have a different horse to sell every three months! Most professional riders sell horses as part of their normal way of life, either because they trade as dealers or because it is part of their living. Some people may assume that buying from a dealer who specializes in show horses automatically means that you will be buying a not quite top class horse, as such a person would want to keep top class prospects. The answer to that is that whilst no showing professional would be likely to want sell a novice prospect that had Wembley champion written all over it, someone who has a constant supply of horses through his or her hands may decide that something has got to go to keep numbers manageable, or that a new prospect is more 'their type' than a previous purchase. It has to be said, too, that even the most knowledgeable people make decisions they later regret, especially when they are standing in a line-up on the wrong side of the horse they sold!

THE DEALER'S VIEWPOINT

Ninety-nine per cent of the horses I sell are cobs, because that's what I'm known for. They vary from potential top class show cobs, including some who have already started their careers in the ring, to nice all-rounders who will show well at riding club or agricultural show level.

The fact that I sell a horse doesn't mean I don't like it. It's my living, and I won't buy any horse if I don't like the look of it. I've sold many cobs that have qualified for and done well at Wembley and one of them was Cob of the Year, so you can't say you're automatically getting second best!

The one thing I can do is give someone a fair assessment of a horse's potential and advise them on whether they'll be able to ride it. That's something a lot of people forget, that it's all very well saying you want to get to Wembley, but not so good if you can't ride one side of your potential star. I've got a handful of top class prospects in my yard at the moment; as three-year-olds, one was so sharp he would have scared a lot of people silly. He'll be fine when he goes in the ring, but that's my job.

You also have to be realistic in what you can achieve. There's nothing wrong in dreaming of winning at the HOYS, but if in the hard light of day you know you're not going to aim higher than a good local or at the most an agricultural show, buy a nice horse that will do well at that level and that you can have fun with.

Lynn Russell

Buying from an auction is an accepted practice in the racing world and on the Continent, where potential dressage horses and show jumpers change hands for huge sums. In this country, auction sales – apart from the specialist bloodstock ones – have tended to have a slightly dodgy image and are often thought of as the place where people get rid of problem horses that they can't sell privately. This may be true in some cases when you are talking about markets at the bottom end of the scale, but at the top end, some very high class horses go under the hammer for some very big prices.

If you are looking for a TB horse to make a hack, riding horse or lightweight hunter, you may be tempted to visit one of the bloodstock sales – but remember that it will be horses for courses. For instance, Tattersalls in Newmarket concentrates on horses for the Flat, which are lighter in build than those bred for National Hunt racing sold at Doncaster.

A lot of good horses have come out of racing, either before or after they have reached the racetrack, and in the right hands have gone on to successful showing careers. However, buying at auction demands a keen eye and a cool nerve. In some cases you will be looking for a racing reject, a horse who is either too slow or has an unfashionable pedigree or both, but although vets are present at the sales, the procedure is not as rigorous as that demanded for the five-stage pre-purchase veterinary procedure.

If you buy from the horses in training section, you also have to be prepared to turn your purchase away for a few months so that the horse can relax and 'let down'.

Briganoon started his career in racing and went on to become a successful small hunter

Racehorses are kept stabled for most of the time and fed large quantities of high energy food, and adapting to the lifestyle of a 'normal' horse can take a little time. There is also a higher percentage of stereotypic behaviour amongst racehorses than others, though animals which weave, crib bite or windsuck have to be described as such in the catalogue.

At any sale, it is important to read the catalogue description and understand what isn't said as well as what is. It is equally important to read the auctioneers' conditions and terms of sale: for instance, at some sales a warranty of soundness may cover wind, eyes, heart and action whilst others omit the heart. So if you bought a horse under the latter stipulation and it dropped dead from heart failure as it walked off the lorry, you would have absolutely no comeback.

The prestige sales do their best to protect buyer and seller and many only accept horses if they go through a full pre-purchase veterinary examination beforehand and another at the sales venue, by the appointed vets, immediately they are sold. Those at the lower end are decidedly more vague; for instance, they may state that details of height, age and breeding given in the catalogue do not count as warranties.

Catalogue descriptions can be literary masterpieces and traps for the unwary. 'Believed to be sound' is an opinion, not a warranty and 'good in light traffic' could mean that the horse goes ballistic if a lorry comes within half a mile. If there is a long list of virtues, you also have to ask yourself if anything is missing: for instance, it might be good to box, catch and clip, but does that mean it is a nightmare to shoe?

This means that if the horse described as a five-year-old turns out to be ten and you did not recognize this when you looked at its teeth, you are stuck with it. Likewise, if the potential show cob catalogued as being within the height limit turns out to be a centimetre over when you get him measured, it is your hard luck. In general, if you buy at auction you need to be very experienced or to have someone with you who is – and to accept that you are taking a gamble. At a prestige sale, you must expect to pay a good price for a good horse. At a more downmarket auction, you might get a bargain or you might buy a problem.

Buying from a private seller has its own pitfalls, ranging from the owner who overestimates the horse's conformation, movement, ability and even height to the person who can't stand the animal they own and will tell you any story to get rid of it. There are also plenty of people who make themselves out to be 'private' sellers when in fact they sell several animals a year and are more accurately described as dealers.

Barrister Julie Mackenzie, author of *Horse Law* (J A Allen, 2001) has this to say: 'The measure of protection for the buyer depends on whether the sale is a private or business sale. A private sale is one between two private individuals. A business sale is where the seller carries on a business of buying and selling horses. Whether a person is a horse dealer and, therefore, conducting a business sale is a question of fact, but even limited selling may be considered dealing and, therefore, a business.'

Perhaps the lesson to be learned here is that if you see the same telephone number appearing regularly and the person claims to be a private seller, be wary. Genuine dealers are quite open about the fact that they sell horses for a living, just as professional riders who sell a percentage of the horses they buy also acknowledge that they are doing this as part of their living. It's the ones who are pregnant three times a year or who are always on the verge of emigrating/selling their houses that should strike a note of caution. Also, a lot of breeders who, understandably and legitimately, sell their stock, have little understanding of the law and may be quite indignant when it is suggested that they are carrying on a business. However, even if they get genuine pleasure from breeding and rearing young horses and very little or no profit when they sell them, the fact that they bred them intending to sell them means that they are operating on business, not private, lines.

General tips for making sure you are not travelling miles to see an unsuitable horse include:

- If the advert does not include a photograph, ask for one before you commit yourself to making the journey.

- Read the advert carefully and assume nothing. 'Good in all respects' might been just that, or it might mean that the seller has forgotten that the horse is bad in traffic. Ask about every issue that concerns you.
- Has the seller measured the horse or is he guessing at the height?
- Is the breeding and age verifiable?
- Does it have any splints, curbs, thoroughpins, bog spavins or curbs? If the seller does not know what any or some of these are, you may have to keep your fingers crossed.

Vetting

When you think you have found your potential show horse, it is well worth having him or her vetted. No matter how knowledgeable you are or how good a judge of conformation, there are some things – such as an eye defect – that only a vet would pick up on. A satisfactory pre-purchase examination also means that you have a certificate to show to an insurance company; if the horse develops a problem that would have shown up during the examination, you have proof that it was not a pre-existing condition when you bought him. If you are buying a horse out of the area covered by your usual practice, ask your vet to recommend someone in that part of the country.

It is important to understand what the vetting procedure means and therefore what you can and cannot expect from the vet who carries it out. It is not a guarantee that the horse is totally defect or problem-free; rather, it is an examination which results in the vet being able to say that on the day, in his or her opinion, the findings were likely or unlikely to affect the animal's purpose for a particular job. That isn't as vague as it sounds, because vets, like everyone else, are subject to rules of professional competence and the five-stage vetting procedure is very thorough.

However, it is not the vet's job to tell you whether or not you have a potential Wembley winner or even a potential show horse. Conformation faults as they might affect performance and blemishes should be noted and discussed with you, but it isn't the vet's job to decide whether you have a future showing star. That decision rests with you and anyone with specialist knowledge that you take with you as an advisor.

When you've bought your horse, you will probably want to insure him – unless you have so many other horses that insurance premiums are not a practical proposition, as happens with many professionals. For the one or two-horse owner, though, insurance against death, theft and straying and for veterinary fees is a good investment. Loss of use cover, where you insure against the possibility of accident or illness preventing the horse from *permanently* being unable to do the job or jobs for which he is insured, sends premiums sky high and is usually impractical with a show horse. For instance, insurance

It is recommended that you have a potential show horse vetted by a good horse vet – in this case, Andy Bathe, now equine surgeon at Cambridge University Veterinary School

companies inevitably specify that if the horse develops a blemish which would count against him in the show ring but does not affect his soundness, they will not pay out.

To avoid misunderstandings and disappointments, read your policy document thoroughly as soon as you get it. Query anything you don't understand, because if you don't, you will be deemed to have accepted the policy terms and conditions.

THE DEALER'S VIEW

Vetting the show horse is always a thorny issue. As someone with a foot bridging two camps – showing and dealing – I'm amazed by the different views and expectations pre-purchase examinations stimulate.

I'm not against vetting: far from it. I won't sell a horse unless the purchaser either has a full five-stage vetting carried out, complete with blood sample, or signs an acknowledgement that I advised them to do so and a disclaimer.

From the buyer's point of view, vetting provides peace of mind and avoids potential disappointment. For me, it means that no one can say a horse has a lump or bump I didn't point out…or even worse, that it was 'on something'.

What does annoy me is if vets ignore the purpose of their examination – to make a clinical examination and give an opinion that, as the vetting form states, 'on the balance of probabilities the conditions set out are/are not likely to prejudice this animal's use' for a particular job. It is not a vet's job to 'fail' a horse because he or she does not think it is a particular type or will not compete successfully at a particular level.

If you want expert advice on whether the horse you're looking at is a good stamp of show cob, or a potential small hack, take someone with you who competes successfully in those categories. Don't expect a vet to decide whether a four-year-old cob will make up to a lightweight or heavyweight or if a hack has enough charisma, or if a growing youngster will exceed the adult height limit.

If your advisor is a professional, expect to pay for his or her time. Don't begrudge it: the only way we learn is by our mistakes. We all make them and they can be very expensive.

Lynn Russell

6 MANAGEMENT ISSUES

It is often said that rosettes are won 99 per cent at home and one per cent in the ring. The way you keep your horse, which includes his accommodation, food and general handling, is a vital part of production. It isn't just doing things 'by the book' or otherwise, it's a matter of horse sense. You have to know your horse or pony as an individual and if he has a bright or complex personality, as is the case with many top class animals in all disciplines, decide how to make this work for you rather than against you.

There are also welfare issues involved in showing, in particular the question of animals which are stuffed with food in order to achieve what their owners fondly call 'show condition' and which in reality is anything but. There are other issues to think about, too. For instance, whilst you will want to do everything possible to avoid your show horse or pony getting injured or blemished, he is still a horse. As a creature of instinct, he has a psychological need to roam and whilst it is impossible for most of us to give our horses as much room as nature intended, we can still provide daily turnout. Most horses are happy to be stabled part of the time and there are plenty who prefer to be in when it is cold, windy and raining – but it is not fair to regularly stable any animal for 23 hours out of 24. This is common practice in the racing industry and is a major reason why so many racehorses show stereotypic behaviour such as weaving or crib biting.

Allowing your show animal the space and time to be a horse, to wander around, graze on appropriate pasture, socialize with others and have a good roll is all part of good management. It applies to everything from a Shetland pony to a hack and recognizing this is one of the secrets of many top producers. Unfortunately, there are still too many cases of show horses who are permanently wrapped up in so many rugs and bandages they can hardly move, usually to keep them clean and get their coats into perfect condition.

We all want our horses to have sleek, shiny summer coats and to hold on to them until the end of the showing season, but it goes beyond the acceptable limits of

Nothing beats going out in the field, as Face the Music, a former champion small hunter, proves

production when native pony enthusiasts cover up ponies bred to be hardy and tough with rugs and hoods at the height of summer, all to keep the coat short and fine. Nor is it fair to permanently stable horses and ponies with naturally laid-back temperaments in order to try and give them more 'sparkle' in the ring.

In the next chapter, we look at trimming techniques. There are some people who believe that pulling manes and tails and trimming off whiskers is cruel, because doing so deprives horses of their natural protection, but as long as you are prepared to compensate for what you take off, your horse should not suffer. Whiskers on the muzzle might be used as 'feelers,' but horses do not seem to notice their loss; fly guards and sheets give protection from biting insects and as long as you leave the hair inside the ear and trim only the outer edges, your horse will not suffer. At the end of the day, if you are totally anti-trimming, you should choose a native pony, as breed societies stipulate minimal or no pulling and trimming.

A good outdoor rug with detachable neck cover, such as this design by Chaskit, can help keep your horse clean

Home from home

In most cases, the best way to keep horses happy is to keep them on some kind of combined system. This usually means turning them out in the daytime and bringing them in at night, though many people prefer to reverse this in really hot weather and stable during the heat of the day and turn out at night, when it is cooler. In either case, make sure that your field offers shelter in cold, wet and windy weather and shade and a refuge from insects at other times of year. Shelter can mean anything from trees and thick hedging to a suitable building.

Similarly, make sure that your stable is a place of comfort and relaxation for your horse, not a badly ventilated, poorly sited trap. Horses, like people, have likes and dislikes; just as some people thrive in bustling cities and find the peace of the countryside oppressive, whilst others hate noise, traffic and crowds, so one horse's ideal home will make another unhappy. Unfortunately, horses don't have a say in where they live – it is our responsibility to try and make sure that we recognize when they are unhappy and do whatever we can to put it right.

EXPERT VIEWS
It's very important to find out what sort of environment suits a particular horse and if your horse is unhappy in the stable, try and find a way round it. They are just as

individual as people – some like to be able to see all that's going on, whilst others prefer peace and quiet. You can make a lot of difference to a horse's well-being and attitude by observing its behaviour and trying to get inside its mind.

For instance, some horses are so anxious not to miss anything that's going on that they will eat a mouthful of food, go to the door, go back to their food and so on. They are often much happier if you give them their hard feed in a manger that hooks over the door and hang haynets so that they can eat and watch at the same time. The opposite of this is the horse who likes peace and quiet in which to eat his food.

We had a top class mare here who was very difficult to settle, but we tried her in various boxes in various parts of the yard until we found a place she was happy with. We're lucky in that our yard is made up of several small groups of boxes rather than being a large, open-plan area. This means we can move horses to quieter or busier places if we think they would prefer it.

All our horses are turned out every day so that they can relax. Sometimes they go out in small, compatible groups, but if a new horse comes in – perhaps for breaking or schooling – we turn it out with a quiet pony to start with. Some people worry about horses hurting themselves or getting dirty, but if being turned out is part of their normal routine they find it relaxing. They might have a buck and a play, but that's all part of being a horse; in any case, you can always put brushing boots on before you turn them out to protect them against accidental knocks.

You can and should take every care to minimize the risk of your horse knocking itself or getting kicked, but you can't wrap show horses up in cotton wool. And as for getting dirty, a good New Zealand, with a neck cover if necessary, takes care of the problem!

Kate Moore

We have three types of 'indoor homes' – ordinary stables, stalls and a small open-fronted barn. With the ordinary stables, we use plastic-covered chains which clip across an open doorway in the daytime so the horses don't feel shut in and get the benefits of extra ventilation. The yard is sheltered, so we don't have to close the doors except at night. Ventilation is really important, it's far better to put on an extra rug than reduce the ventilation by closing the door because you're worried the horse will get cold.

A lot of people are horrified by the idea of stalls but horses are very happy in them, because they are reassured by the close presence of horses on each side. Our stalls enable the horses to look out and they are on a 'log and rope' arrangement which gives them the freedom to lie down – a rope with a wooden ball on the end passes through a ring and clips to the headcollar, which is much less restrictive than if the horses are tied up in the ordinary way. If you own a horse that weaves, you'll find it doesn't do it in a stall, which proves that they are happy this way.

No horse is stabled or stands in a stall all the time, unless of course it has to be confined because of an injury. They all go out in the field in compatible pairs or small groups, whether they are top class show horses or dealing animals. I prefer to have geldings, both for myself and to sell, as this makes turning horses out much easier.

The barn is brilliant, as it means we can turn two or three compatible horses out in it in bad weather. They have enough room to wander around and because it's so well ventilated we can use straw. In the stables and stalls, we use rubber matting, which works well because we have good drainage. It's comfortable for the horses and economical, as it saves on labour and time.

Lynn Russell

Our show ponies are turned out to play every day, either in the field or in our 'play pen' – a small area where we turn out one or two at a time. Mares in particular seem to thrive on being turned out: it helps them chill out! We don't let them down completely at the end of the season, though – show ponies are not like natives, they're not designed to run out on the hills.

Penny Hollings

A stable should be a haven, not a prison

Feeding

Feeding the show horse is a highly contentious area. It is also no exaggeration to say that it is a serious welfare issue, as was proved when the International League for the Protection of Horses took in a four-year-old which was potentially a top class show hunter, but had been crippled with laminitis through overfeeding. Despite the efforts of its staff and the ILPH farrier, John Brake, it was eventually decided that the horse would not stay sound enough even for light work and it was put down.

This may have been an extreme case, but there are still far too many overweight show horses in the ring. 'Show condition' is often a euphemism for fat, though many professional producers and judges say that they are trying to get the message across that a show horse needs to be reasonably fit. Whilst a show animal will never be as fit and lean as an event or endurance horse, it should not be a barrel of lard on legs.

So what is ideal condition? In general terms, it means that the horse has no excess fat deposits, has good muscle tone and is able to move in a free, athletic way. You should be able to feel the ribs but not see them – though admittedly with particularly good doers, such as cobs, this may not be as easy as with a thin skinned, TB show hack! The horse should be bright and alert without being on the verge of exploding because it is overfed and underworked.

If you find it hard to assess your own horse or want a more scientific method, use condition scoring. This defines horses in various stages and numbers each from 0, very poor, to 5, very fat. Ideally you should aim for 3, denoting good condition, but sadly there are still many horses in the ring who could only be categorized as 4 or even 5. These are the scoring levels and what they mean:

0   Very poor. The overall impression is that the horse's skin is stretched tight over its skeleton; ribs, pelvis and even backbone will be prominent and the horse has a sunken rump, often with a cavity under the tail. It will look as if it has ewe (upside down) neck.

1   Poor. The horse shows the same signs as before, to a slightly less marked degree.

2   Moderate. The ribs are just visible, but not the backbone. The rump is flat, not rounded and the neck firm but narrow.

3   Good. The ribs are covered and cannot be seen, but can be felt without any pushing or prodding. The neck is firm but there is no fatty crest.

4   Fat. It is difficult or impossible to feel the ribs and pelvis and there is a 'gutter' along the back. The neck may be starting to look a bit cresty, but this is fat, not correct muscle development.

Use a weightape to
monitor your horse's
condition

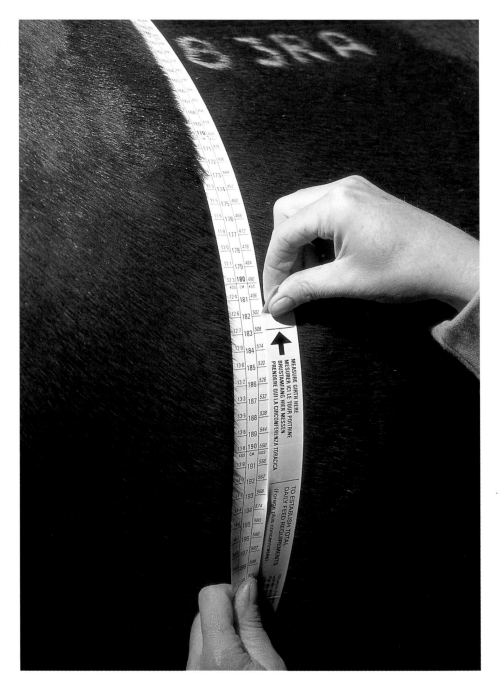

5   Very fat. The ribs cannot be felt and there is a deep gutter along the back. The
    rump bulges and there is a pronounced fatty crest to the neck. You can get hold
    of pads and rolls of fat, for instance on the shoulder and crest.

EXPERT TIP

When you are carrying out a condition score assessment, you're scoring for fat cover only. Horses store fat on their necks, over their shoulders, backbones and ribs and on their rumps – not on their underbellies. The easiest way to score is to divide the horse into three sections and feel for fat cover on each one in turn. Give each area a score out of five, as explained above, then note the average score. Get into the habit of doing this regularly.

Teresa Hollands, nutritionist for Dodson and Horrell

Unfortunately, a lot of showing people work on the theory that fat covers a multitude of sins. In fact, the opposite is true: any judge worth his or her salt will be able to see through the blubber. Even more important, obesity puts a strain on a horse's heart, lungs and limbs that may well have a permanent effect, especially in the case of overweight youngstock shown in-hand. If you want to see youngstock in good condition, look at those produced by experts such as John and Sue Rawding, who have been breeding and producing show horses for many years and win numerous champ-ionships without overfeeding.

The risk of laminitis has already been mentioned. Contrary to popular belief, this is not a disease which only affects little fat ponies: ponies and animals with pony or draught blood may be statistically more at risk, because they have evolved to live on what we regard as poor grazing and to walk many miles each day looking for food. However, horses with a high percentage of Thoroughbred or Arab blood can also be victims.

A show horse has to move well and be athletic. That means, by definition, that it has to be reasonably fit and in healthy but not fat condition, as fat restricts the shoulders and therefore the movement. A fat horse does not walk, it waddles; you will often hear it said that cobs are naturally poor walkers, but this does not have to be the case. A cob that is too wide and 'bosomy' will have a rolling gait, but a correctly made cob that is not grossly overweight will have a decent walk.

EXPERT VIEWS

When you look at a line-up of show horses, you'll nearly always see that the ones at the head of it are well-covered but – and this is the important thing – they are correctly muscled, not fat. A lot of people still confuse the two and are so anxious to get a good topline on the horse that they stuff it full of food. You have to feed a horse properly to get it in the right shape, but you also have to work it correctly. If you pat one of my cobs on the neck you'll feel hard muscle, not a wobbly lump of blubber.

A horse with good conformation is well made whether it's fat or thin and the same applies to one with conformation faults. Don't kid yourself that putting weight on a second rate horse will hide a multitude of sins and turn it into a top class one. It won't...and you won't fool the judge! When I'm judging, the last thing I want is to get on a cob and feel as if I'm doing the splits.

Lynn Russell

The issue of overweight show horses is still a serious one. I know that judges have no option but to judge what's in front of them and if you have a class full of fat horses you have no option but to place them. But I do think it would be a good thing if more judges told exhibitors that their horses were too fat. People are only going to listen if you hit them where it hurts, through the rosettes.

Jo Jenkins, show producer

By producing an animal in an overweight condition you are doing a disservice not only to its health but to its potential as a show horse. Overweight horses and ponies cannot use the full range of movement of the shoulder, with a detrimental effect on the paces, nor can they achieve their maximum athleticism.

Some people believe that a fat, unfit animal will be calmer and easier to ride and manage than a fitter one. In fact, the opposite is true: fat horses tire easily when asked to work, as do their muscles, and in trying to avoid discomfort they become more stressed. This in turn can lead to what the rider may think of as bad behaviour but is in fact the horse saying 'I can't do this.'

Davina Whiteman, former leading show rider and chairman
of Ponies Association (UK)

A JUDGE'S VIEW

I do think things have improved over the past couple of years because there has been so much written in the equestrian press about this issue and a lot of vets have made their feelings clear. As a judge, I don't like to see horses that are much too fat and I certainly don't like riding them. They're uncomfortable, they waddle and it restricts their wind.

Cob exhibitors are the worst offenders, probably because these horses are naturally such good doers. That's no excuse for letting your horse turn into a tub of lard, though. The working hunters are usually the best of the bunch, because a fat horse can't jump as well as a fit one. Hopefully the message that fit is better than flabby is filtering down through the other sections.

It both amuses me and annoys me when people say 'I've got to have my horse fat because that's what the judges like, or they wouldn't place them.' That's like trying to decide which came first, the chicken or the egg. If you've got a class consisting almost entirely of fat horses in front of you then it's inevitable that some of them will be in the frame – and if there is a horse that is streets ahead of the competition but is overweight, what do you do?

Realistically, you can't turn round to someone and tell them that you like their horse but you're not going to place it because it's too fat. What I do is tell them that I like the horse but would like it even more if it carried less weight. If enough judges do the same, and I think that is happening, we may see even more improvement.

Show horses are always going to be fatter than, say, event horses. It's a different game and a different job. But if you get a class of show hunters who are puffing and blowing after they've trotted round the ring, you do ask yourself what they would be like trying to do the real thing.

Feeding strategies

Once you are clear about the condition you are aiming to get, or keep, your horse in, you need to work out a feeding strategy. The basics of this will be the same whether you are feeding a show hack or a mountain and moorland pony, because they all evolved the same way and have the same digestive system! What will vary is the horse's temperament and whether or not it is a good doer.

Horses evolved to eat forage, not cereals. They are naturally 'trickle feeders' who are designed by nature to eat for most of the day, not to have long periods between meals. This means that the best way to keep a show horse – or any horse – is to allow plenty of time in the field, restricting grazing when necessary. Either strip graze, using electric fencing to partition your field into small areas that can be grazed down rather than allowing unlimited access to rich grass, or try one of the muzzles that permit the horse to graze but limit the amount he can take in. In other words, make him work for his food.

Keeping your horse out in the daytime and stabled at night – reversing this if necessary in really hot weather – should allow him the best of both worlds. If he is thin skinned, use one of the mesh rugs designed to keep off flies; a fly guard or mask will be appreciated by all horses but particularly by hogged cobs. A lightweight sheet will also help if you are trying to prevent colour being bleached out by the sun, for example in the case of a palomino. Whatever you do, don't lose sight of the fact that he is a horse first and a show animal second.

Forage, which includes grass, hay, haylage and 'forage feeds' made from oat and barley straw and/or quick-dried alfalfa and grass, should make up at least 75 per cent of your horse or pony's diet. If this is not enough to provide enough fuel and keep him in good condition, you will need to add hard feed. For most people, the easiest and most efficient way is to choose cubes or coarse mix made by a reputable manufacturer.

To work out how much to feed your horse, you first need to know his bodyweight. The only really reliable way is to use a properly calibrated weighbridge, found at many large veterinary practices and racing yards, but as not many of us have regular access to these the next best thing is a weightape. Weightapes are a rough guide more than a measure of accuracy, but using one once a fortnight will show you whether your horse is maintaining, losing or gaining weight.

And although it might sound obvious, stand back and look at your horse. Can you no longer feel his ribs now that the spring grass has come through? Are his hip bones more prominent after a few weeks of colder weather? Is he so full of himself that he is being silly, or has he become lethargic? We all feel less energetic in hot weather, but if lethargy and weight loss are combined and you are sure that the horse is not ill, you may need to increase his feed or change the hard feed you are using to one with a higher energy level.

There is no such thing as a foolproof feeding regime for all horses, but there are golden rules that should be applied to the show horse or pony as well as to any other.

- Make sure that your horse's mouth and teeth are in good condition. If they are not, he will not be able to chew properly and will not get the full value from his food – plus he will be uncomfortable in his mouth and probably resistant. Likewise, make sure you get your vet's advice on a good worming programme for your individual situation and pick up droppings from the field as often as possible, preferably daily. Drug manufacturers usually suggest programmes and dosing intervals but these can only be general: if you keep two horses at home on well-managed grazing you will not need to follow the same regime as if your horse is on a large yard with a constantly changing equine population. This is one of the rare occasions when your vet can save you money!
- Feed according to age, bodyweight and workload. Young, growing horses and older animals have different nutritional requirements.
- At least 75 per cent of the daily intake should be good quality forage.
- Add one tablespoon of table salt to your horse's diet each day.
- Feed some form of succulent when grazing is in short supply. Succulents include soaked sugar beet pulp, carrots and apples.
- Manufacturers give 'recommended' feeding quantities but these are inevitably general and usually on the high side. If you feed less than 3kg day of nuts or coarse mix, you may need to add a broad spectrum vitamin and mineral

supplement. Good feed companies have nutritionists who will give free advice, albeit based on their own products.

- If you want to feed oats, a traditional feed for horses, rather than a commercial feed, you will also need to feed an oat balancer to make up for deficiencies.
- Increase work before you increase feed, not vice versa. Feed according to the work you are doing, not what you plan to do.
- You can't change a horse's temperament through feeding: 'competition mix' won't turn a laid-back individual into a rocket on four legs. However, you can minimize problems by the way you feed: see the problems and solutions section at the end of this chapter.
- Make sure that your horse always has clean, fresh water.
- Buy top quality feed and forage. Never feed dusty or mouldy hay and if you open a bale of haylage and find mould, discard the whole bale. Good suppliers will replace any faulty ones.

EXPERT VIEWS

Horses have evolved to eat forage, so their digestive system is designed to cope with it best. It also satisfies appetite, requires lots of chewing – thus keeping the horse occupied – and promotes a high production of saliva, which in itself helps to keep the digestive system functioning normally. You should always feed at least one per cent of the bodyweight as forage to keep your horse healthy, and preferably more.

The problem is that forage is nutritionally variable. Growth stage, plant species, soil characteristics and weather conditions at harvest are variable factors that affect nutrient content. This must be taken into account when formulating the overall diet; for instance, in the case of a 15.2hh horse eating 8kg hay per day, changing hay could mean a huge increase in protein and energy intake. You would need to drop the hard feed dramatically to maintain this horse's bodyweight.

Treat your pasture as a crop, not just a turnout area, and look after it! Horses can eat about 1 to 1.5kg herbage on a dry matter basis per hour of grazing, equivalent to about 5 to 7kg fresh weight. Compared to other feeds, regular grazing pasture provides a medium energy, relatively high protein feed.

The nutrient content of hay depends more on the stage of maturity when it is cut and the weather conditions after cutting than the plant species. Hay varies widely in nutrient content, but is usually low in energy and protein. If in doubt, have it analyzed.

Haylage is richer in nutrients than hay made from the same herbage and is dust free

Haylage made
especially for horses
is an excellent
source of dust and
mould-free fibre

and almost mould-free. Look for a dry matter content of over 60 per cent and use within a few days of opening. Avoid haylage that is so rich you can only feed a little.

Grass and alfalfa nuts can be useful, but take less chewing, so the horse takes less time to eat them and less saliva is produced. Soaked down, they are a useful source of fibre and protein for older horses and ponies with poor teeth.

Feed quick-dried forages as if they were grass from pasture. They are much richer in nutrients than hay, although they are light in weight, so 1kg is a full bucketful. Clean oat straw, if you can get it, is very useful for good doers and overweight animals, as it is low in calories. You need to make sure that your horse's teeth are in good condition, introduce it gradually – as with all new feeds – and make sure fresh water is always available, as your horse will probably drink more.

Clare MacLeod, senior nutritionist for Feedmark

Mountain and moorland ponies are 'outdoor animals'. They need to spend most of their time turned out, obviously with adequate shelter. When people stable them too much, they get problems, the ponies become stressed and may develop stable vices such as weaving. We had a lovely pony who unfortunately ended up with someone who kept her stabled 23 hours out of 24; she was dreadfully unhappy and started weaving. We eventually bought her back, but although she became much more settled and relaxed when she was turned out with the other ponies she was never happy when stabled.

Most ponies are perfectly happy kept on a combined system, but you have to be very careful with the way you manage your grazing and get expert advice on the way you look after it and fertilize it from someone who understands native ponies' requirements. You don't want to use nitrogen on it or you'll get a sudden flush of rich grass, which can spark off laminitis. Good forage should be the basis of any horse or pony's diet and in many cases may be all a pony needs unless it is working really hard.

Anne Rolinson, mountain and moorland judge and Connemara breeder.

When the show ponies are stabled we like to feed hay rather than haylage. One reason is that you can feed more of it and so stop them getting bored, and the other is that there is less risk of spoiled bales.

Apart from this, otherwise we feed a basic diet of dampened bran, Dengie Hi-Fi and either Spillers High Fibre cubes or Baileys No 2 cubes. We don't feed sugar beet because we don't want to give extra sugar and in general we don't feed supplements, though some ponies have garlic.

The basic rule is to look at what you're dealing with. We don't have our ponies overly fit, but nor do we want them fat because of the risk of laminitis. We'll probably have them with a bit more weight on to start the season because you don't know how they're going to react to travelling, but we definitely don't have them fat – as soon as we think anything is starting to look a bit porky we cut back.

Penny Hollings

Supplements

There is a huge range of feed supplements on the market now, ranging from herbal calming products to those formulated to help mobility. Whilst there are plenty of products which are undoubtedly of value, the supplements market is also big business...so before you get carried away by the persuasive advertising copy, look at your horse and decide whether he really needs extra help or whether you're buying dreams.

Although supplements – in particular, herbal ones – seem to be a modern phenomenon, in one way they are perhaps trying to make up for deficiencies in modern pasture. At one time, grazing would be seeded especially for horses and meadows would mature over the years with a variety of plants and herbs. Today, a lot of grassland is sown for cattle, whose requirements are very different from those of horses. Grazing for cattle, particularly dairy cattle, is far 'richer' than horses need and can consequently cause problems.

Whereas the fields of bygone years would have lots of plants for horses to pick at or ignore as they chose, including comfrey and dandelions, modern seed mixtures are designed to produce grass. That doesn't mean there is anything wrong with them, simply that if you want your horse to eat particular herbs you need to provide them in a different way. Whether or not they need them is a debate far too long to enter into here, but there are undoubtedly horses which benefit from herbal supplements.

The two basic, straightforward additions to a ration which all horses can benefit from are ordinary table salt, fed at a level of one tablespoon per day, and garlic. Salt makes up for any lost through sweat and according to Andy Bathe, former vet to the British three-day event team, is just as and usually more effective than expensive electrolytes. Garlic is reputed to have astringent properties, to help the respiratory system and to deter flies by altering the smell of the horse's skin and sweat. As long as you don't kiss your horse, it shouldn't cause you any problems!

Herbal calmers are big business and some definitely help some horses. They also help some riders by giving them the confidence that their horse is going to be more relaxed, thus allowing them to relax themselves. We don't fully understand how herbs work, but the fact that herbal medicine has been around for thousands of years must stand for something. And if it works, why knock it?

There are two things to be very careful about with herbal products. One is that although they are marketed with attractive labels such as 'natural,' natural does not necessarily mean harmless. When fed according to the manufacturers' instructions, you should not have any problems, but just as you wouldn't take six aspirin instead of two and expect them to be three times more effective, so you should not exceed the recommended dose on herbal supplements. Nor should you mix them without checking with the manufacturers that one will not conflict with another.

Supplements to maintain joint health and improve flexibility have become incredibly popular. Some people swear by their efficacy whilst others notice no difference. The only certainty is that they should never be used as a substitute for veterinary advice and treatment if you think your horse has a problem – and if you are thinking of using something as a preventive measure, it is worth asking your vet's advice.

Similarly, there are a lot of products to promote the growth of healthy hoof horn. Many are backed with convincing testimonials and your vet or farrier may have advice. As with all supplements, don't expect instant miracles. It will probably be at least three months before you notice a difference in the quality of your horse's feet – and they are no substitute for a good farrier.

Feed balancers are relatively new and advertisements often give you the impression that they are miracles in a bag. But as one major feed company nutritionist puts it: if your horse's basic diet is correct, a feed balancer won't make much difference. If it's lacking, you may indeed notice a better quality coat, weight gain and so on.

Producing a horse with a gleaming, healthy coat has a basis of correct feeding. As Lynn Russell puts it, 'What you put inside is much more important than what you do on the outside.' Boiled linseed is the traditional way of enhancing a coat and many producers still feed it, though as boiling is a slow, potentially messy business and some manufacturers now produce linseed in a ready to feed version, you may prefer to use a modern version of an old favourite.

'Nagsmen's' recipes for a healthy coat include feeding a tablespoon of sulphur powder once a day for five days when the horse is shedding its winter coat and feeding chopped, dried nettles to bring out the dapples in a bay coat.

Problems, problems...

Feeding horses by the book is all very well, but if the horse hasn't read that particular one you might occasionally have problems. The good news is that there are always answers – it's a case of remembering the guidelines and also remembering that every horse is an individual. Here are some of the commonest problems and ways of dealing with them that work...as always, miracles are in short supply and you have to look at feeding as part of your overall management regime.

Temperament problems fall into two distinct categories, the horse who is fizzy and 'over the top' and the opposite side of the coin, the one who seems dull and lazy. If you've got one, you probably wish you had the other to cope with, but both can be frustrating.

One thing you have to accept is that you can't change what's fixed. Nothing is going to turn a sharp, sensitive TB into a bombproof patent safety, or transform a horse who is so laid-back he's almost horizontal into a ball of fire. However, you should be able to bring about an improvement in both cases, provided you have the necessary riding ability. This applies particularly to the sharp horse. Sensitive horses need sensitive riders who can instil confidence and be firm, but calm. Be honest with yourself: if you're as tight as a coiled spring and see your life flash before your eyes every time you get on it, you're probably not going to make perfect partners. No matter how nice the horse, unless you can get help from a sympathetic professional and are prepared to put the idea of competing on the back burner until you are much more confident, you are better off finding the horse a new home and yourself a more compatible mount.

Lazy horses are often easier to deal with – a lot are labelled as idle or ungenerous when they simply have never been taught to go off the leg and have become desensitized to perhaps a succession of riders continually flapping their legs. Again, if you find this type of horse so exasperating you're tempted to lose your temper, forget it. The horse will probably become more introverted and you'll go backwards instead of forwards.

In both cases, feeding can play an important role in solving the problem. Fizzy horses are sometimes difficult to keep weight on, with the result that their owners pile in more and more food and keep a vicious circle going round. With this type of horse, make sure it has plenty of forage and add calories through slow release energy sources: vegetable oil is excellent and is also cheap. Turn the horse out as much as possible, as good grass will put weight on more effectively than anything else and grazing will help to relax him. Haylage is more palatable than hay and if your horse is a picky feeder as well as being fizzy, he is more likely to eat it.

Soaked sugar beet pulp is another good form of slow release energy, though some people swear that it 'hypes up' their horses. The scientific answer to this is that there is absolutely nothing in it that could do this and the only answer is that adding sugar beet tips the overall energy levels in the diet too far and it's easier to blame the sugar beet. Again, horses are individuals, not scientists and if eliminating it from your horse or pony's diet solves a problem, so be it.

THE EXPERT VIEW
Sugar has had a 'bad press' in horse nutrition that is not wholly deserved. This has come from the low sugar and healthy eating trends in certain lines of human foods, and from claims from the holistic fraternity that 'added sugar is not compatible with the evolved physiology of horses'.

This leads to all of us getting comments at talks, shows and on feed helplines regarding the sugar levels in our (Spillers') diets and also claims from some customers that horses are allergic to molasses. Allergy experts do not implicate sugar in horse feed allergies: these are usually a result of a reaction to protein in the cereals.

Studies of sugar digestion in the horse have shown them to digest sugar really easily. This is not surprising, as the horse evolved to eat grass and other pasture plants which are naturally high in sugar. As a result, the horse has developed a sweet tooth – which is why we enhance the palatability of feeds by adding molasses products and even sugar beet pulp.

As the sugar is digested so efficiently in the small intestine, it is unlikely that much, if any, passes to the large intestine. It is therefore unlikely that, as the holistic lobby would suggest, bowel function will be impaired. Bowel function is only likely to be impaired if a large dose of sugar is suddenly administered without any prior adaptation, such as when ponies are turned out for the first time on to lush spring grass.

It is also important to remember that it is the purest form of sugar, glucose, that is the only 'food' the brain uses in order to function – so no glucose, no brain!

Ruth Bishop, Spillers Horse Feeds

Other ways of tempting fussy feeders include adding sliced apples and carrots to the diet and dampening it with water used to soak sugar beet or diluted peppermint cordial. If your horse is reluctant to eat more than tiny amounts, this could be where a feed balancer would be useful.

It's even more important to feed the fussy or hyper horse small meals, often; try and give a feed last thing at night and make it slightly larger than the others. Make sure the horse always has the chance to eat its meals in peace and without feeling threatened by its next door neighbour or the bustle of a busy yard.

Horses can use up to ten per cent of the fuel they get from their food just to keep warm, so make sure that the fizzy horse is always warm enough. It's cheaper to put on a warmer rug than to increase the amount of food.

With the lazy horse, you need quick release energy sources and it's better to feed a small amount of a high energy feed than a larger amount of a low energy one. Alternatively, add a total of up to 1kg oats to his ration. Feed companies usually take the official line that adding extras to cubes and coarse mixes that have been carefully formulated will unbalance the ration, but many nutritionists agree that adding up to 1kg oats should not cause problems. What you don't want to do is play around feeding half a scoop of nuts and half a scoop of barley in one feed, then alfalfa in the next to 'give him a change' and so on. Horses don't get bored eating the same thing – have you ever known a horse or pony get fed up with grazing?

The other common problem is the horse who seems to live on fresh air. This applies mainly to cobs and mountain and moorland ponies and is often associated with the risk of laminitis – so follow the usual preventive measures such as strip grazing. You have to keep these horses and ponies happy by allowing them to eat as nature intended, little and often, but at the same time make them work for their food.

Using a small mesh haynet or putting one ordinary haynet inside another to give the same effect should help slow down the eating rate, as will putting a large, smooth stone in the manger. There are several low energy, high fibre forage feeds available now that are light in weight but high in volume – 1kg nuts is only a standard feed scoop full, but 1kg of, say, a high fibre chop is a bucketful. If you want to keep your fatty happy while other horses are eating, give him a small amount of a feed such as this and/or apples and carrots.

Good doers need their essential nutrients just as much as any other horse. You will certainly be feeding less than the compound feed manufacturers' minimum amount – usually about 3kg daily – to supply vitamins and minerals, so add a broad spectrum vitamin and mineral supplement to make up for it.

Some horses, particularly young ones unaccustomed to travelling and the sights and sound of the showground, may become excited and overstressed until they learn what life is all about. This can cause anything from mild diarrhoea to weight loss and such horses may benefit from probiotics. In simple terms, the horse's guts – like ours – contain a mixture of bacteria, some necessary and beneficial and others which have a negative effect. In times of stress, the 'baddies' can take over from the 'goodies': a probiotic, which literally means 'for life,' can help restore the balance.

There are many good commercial probiotics available through feed manufacturers, or you could add live yoghurt to your horse's feed. I have done this very successfully with an ex-racehorse, who preferred strawberry and black cherry flavours! Some feeds now contain Yea-Sacc, which is not a probiotic but a yeast and creates a good environment for the fibre-digesting bacteria in the hindgut to multiply.

Dental care, worming and farriery

Dental care
A good horse vet with a recognition of the importance of dental care, or a specialist equine dental technician, is an important member of your 'back-up team'. Although

A good horse dentist can both prevent and solve problems

many vets now realize that dental care is a speciality in itself, it has to be said that there is still the occasional practitioner who thinks the whole issue is overhyped and a quick rasp without using a dental gag is sufficient. Equally, you have to be careful to choose a dental technician who is fully trained and accept that if a horse needs to be sedated, this must be carried out by a vet.

Dental problems affect the way the way the horse chews and utilizes his food and also the way he accepts – or does not accept – the bit, so a check-up every six months should be part of your horse's routine management. Horses' teeth are constantly erupting and being ground down as they eat. At least, that is the theory. In practice, the modern domesticated horse spends less time eating than he is designed to and a lot of the food he eats is softer and takes less chewing than would be the case in the wild. This means that nature's way of creating correct occlusion, where upper and lower cheek teeth come together properly, no longer functions and you get sharp points, or hooks, which need to be rasped smooth.

Another dental basic is the removal of wolf teeth, shallow-rooted, vestigial pre-molars that sit just in front of the cheek teeth. They can be found in the upper or lower jaw and, contrary to a popular misconception, in mares as well as geldings. They have no practical value to the horse but can cause interference with the bit, so it makes sense to have them taken out. This is a simple job that, depending on the individual, may or may not call for the horse to be sedated.

Some dentistry experts now like to create a bit seat, which involves rounding the first cheek teeth. Practitioners say that although the bit sits in the interdental space, the convenient gap in the horse's mouth where there are no teeth, when pressure is put on the rein and therefore to one side of the mouth, the bit will bring the corner of the cheek into contact with the first cheek tooth on that side. If that cheek tooth has a sharp point, the horse will obviously be uncomfortable or even in pain, but if the cheek tooth is rounded, he will be more comfortable.

THE VET'S VIEW

The veterinary profession has certainly become more aware of the importance of dentistry, which can only be a good thing. However, it is important to look at horses as individuals, not assume that, for instance, a bit seat is essential for every horse. You also need to remember that procedures only work if they are carried out correctly and a badly done bit seat can cause more problems than it prevents.

I now advise owners to have their horses checked twice a year and if, in between times, they think they may have a problem to call me out there and then rather than wait for the next routine visit. It isn't a good idea for owners to poke around inside horses' mouths, because unless you have a properly adjusted gag there is a big danger that you could get badly bitten.

However, there are warning signs that owners can watch out for which indicate that a horse needs attention. These include resistances whilst being ridden, such as head tilting or general 'gobbiness,' an aversion to firm pressure being put on the outside of the face over the teeth and quidding, or dropping food whilst eating.

Horses have 24 cheek teeth and the outside edges of the upper ones can get very sharp, to the extent that they cut the inside of the cheeks. This is obviously painful and can cause ulcers. It's amazing how many professional and supposedly knowledgeable riders begrudge the time and money spent on dental care and think that the answer is simply to pull the noseband tighter; in my experience, the so-called amateur owners are much more prepared to get regular, qualified advice and check-ups.

THE NUTRITIONIST'S VIEW

The old saying that 'You are what you eat' applies as much to your horse as it does to you. The first rule of feeding is that the horse has to be able to eat the food in the first place!

Once food has been picked up or, as in the case of grazing, torn off, it passes to the back of the mouth and is ground by the molars. This starts off the digestive process by breaking food into tiny particles and exposing it to saliva – but horses only produce saliva when they chew, and lack of saliva can lead to gastric ulcers in horses on low-forage diets.

Get your horse to eat from as natural a position as possible, in other words with his head on the ground. This helps keep the natural rotation of the jaw as that of a grazing horse and can thus help reduce the number of hooks and sharp edges on the teeth.

Ruth Bishop, Spillers Horse Feeds

Worming

Worming is another vital weapon not only in enabling your horse to make the most of his food, but in protecting his health. A heavy parasite burden can lead to poor condition, a staring coat, lethargy and potentially fatal colic.

The right drug programme coupled with effective pasture management will minimize risks. The past few years have seen new anti-worming drugs developed that make life easier, but it is important to base your routine on the advice of a knowledgeable equine vet who knows your horses and the way you keep them. Drug companies offer suggested routines and dosing intervals, but this advice is inevitably general.

Consulting your vet rather than diving straight in with a generalized programme can save you money – and as most vets will admit, that doesn't often happen! It will also help to ensure that you do not waste money, encourage resistance or harm the environment by worming too often. We know that there is widespread resistance to the benzimidazole group of wormers and that drug residues in droppings may kill insects and earthworms that are either useful or provide food for other useful species.

By targeting your programme to your horses and your circumstances, you can protect your horse without causing problems. For instance, the owner of two horses kept at home on well-managed grazing can follow a different plan to the owner or client of a large yard with a constantly changing horse population.

Pasture management is just as vital. One of the most effective ways to beat worms is to remove droppings as often as possible, preferably every day. If your field is too large

Don't ignore the necessity of worming: this worm burden was present in a healthy looking show horse just over from Ireland

to make this feasible, use a paddock sweeper – expensive but a good investment for a large yard because of the time and labour it saves – or a chain harrow. Only harrow when the weather is hot, dry and sunny, as ultraviolet light helps to destroy the worm larvae: harrowing in the wrong conditions simply spreads eggs and larvae around and compounds the problem

Most worms are species specific, so taking horses off the field and grazing with cattle or sheep for short periods reduces the risks and also helps maintain your grazing. Cattle can poach the land in wet weather, but eat the longer grass horses don't like, whilst sheep prefer shorter grass but 'pat down' the land instead of damaging it - so the ideal routine would be to graze with cattle for a few weeks in the summer, and with sheep in winter.

Farriery

Most of us think of farriers as an expensive and necessary evil, no matter how nice they are. But a good farrier can be one of the best allies a showing enthusiast can have, so make routine visits a must. Even if your horse does little roadwork, don't leave more than six weeks between bookings; that way, you will ensure that your horse's feet stay correctly balanced and that he stays sound.

Ponies, especially the small ones, can be shown unshod but you may find this does not work if they are doing roadwork. Even if your pony does not need shoes, he needs his feet checking and trimming every six weeks to maintain the correct foot balance.

EXPERT VIEWS

A good farrier is worth his weight in gold, so if you find one, hang on to him and make sure you've always got the kettle boiling when he arrives! Even if he isn't particularly interested in or knowledgeable about showing, he can help make the most of your horse's conformation and movement and – even more important – help keep him sound.

Most show horses are fine with normal weight shoes. Some people like to use lightweight aluminium ones on show hacks to try and get as much extravagance as possible in the action, but these are expensive. In general, take your farrier's advice on which weight of shoe would be best for your horse, bearing in mind that heavier types such as cobs need heavier shoes.

During the show season, I like to have stud holes put in hind shoes and with extravagant movers, in front ones as well. This means you can use studs whenever the ground conditions are less than perfect and be confident that your horse won't slip. Nothing destroys a horse's confidence quicker than worrying that it can't keep its feet.

A show horse should by definition have good or at least adequate movement, but a good farrier can enhance movement and appearance. For instance, if your horse turns its toes in slightly, offsetting the toeclips in front gives the optical illusion that it stands straighter than it actually does. Similarly, if a horse moves slightly close, feathering the inside edge so that it is higher and narrower than the outside one will encourage the foot outwards from the normal line of flight. Horses can't wear protective boots in the ring, except during the jumping phase of a working hunter class, so this can minimize the risk of damage.

You may find that a young horse, particularly one with extravagant movement, tends to overreach when it is tired or excited. This means that it hits the back of the front foot with the front of the back one, which can cause wounds that are difficult to heal. Your farrier may be able to help, perhaps by shoeing the horse with rolled toes and setting the hind shoes well back.

One thing you can't expect a farrier to do, however brilliant he is at his job, is to change the basic way in which a horse goes. Movement involves the whole limb and shoulder and to try and 'straighten' the action of a mature horse puts strain on the limbs. This also proves how important it is to have young horses' feet trimmed well and regularly.

Lynn Russell

Show ponies are often shod with aluminium plates in front and lightweight steel shoes behind, to enhance their elegant movement. Larger ponies and those who hack out a lot, or jump, may need steels all round, with stud holes if required.

Nigel Hollings

Many exhibitors like to use screw-in studs for extra security, particularly on wet going, so you will need to ask your farrier to supply shoes with stud holes. As a general guideline, square studs are used for soft going and pointed ones when the ground is hard. At one time many people only used one stud per shoe, in the outside heel, but it is generally agreed that this can unbalance the foot and that it is far better to use two studs per shoe, one in each heel.

They should only be used when actually competing, not for hacking out and certainly not when travelling, when there is a risk that the horse can catch or stand on the opposite coronet band and cause a serious puncture wound. When the studs are taken out, it is important to plug the holes either with cotton wool soaked in hoof oil or flat-topped 'blanks' to prevent dirt and grit getting in.

7 GETTING THE LOOK

If you have ever seen a top class show horse on its winter holiday, or seen a novice prospect in the raw, you'll realize how much difference skilful trimming, pulling and plaiting can make. Although you can't make a silk purse out of a sow's ear, you can present a horse to its best advantage, making the most of all its good points and minimizing any not so good ones. In some situations you can even create an optical illusion by, for instance, setting plaits at a particular height on the neck or hogging a cob at just the right time before a show.

Before you get out the clippers and the plaiting thread, there are two important first steps. One is to stand back and make an honest assessment of your horse, comparing what you see to the ideal picture. If you feel you can't do this, ask someone knowledgeable to help. Some people find it easier to take photographs of their horse and look at these rather than at the real thing, but this only works if you can take a decent picture.

Try and pick up on all the little details. Could your horse be very slightly light of bone for his body? If so, this will affect the way you trim his legs. Are his hocks not quite perfect? Then you may want to leave his tail a little longer. Don't expect to fool a good judge – but judges accept that presentation is all part of the game.

The other essential is to check the rules and regulations of relevant breed societies and organizations; this applies particularly to Arabs and mountain and moorlands, which are supposedly shown in a natural state with full manes and tails and untrimmed limbs. However, the definitions of 'natural' are in many cases fairly flexible, especially in the mountain and moorland world.

For instance, breeds such as the Exmoor, Fell, Dales and Highland must not be trimmed or have their manes and tails pulled. There has been a lot of heated discussion about this, as there are practical and welfare issues at stake: for instance, if a pony's tail is allowed to grow completely unchecked, there may be times when the pony treads on the tail or it gets balled up with snow in harsh conditions. Another view to consider is that for breeds to survive, they have to be able to perform.

Welsh breeds are trimmed: in theory, discreetly. However, when the head of a champion Welsh pony appears on the front of *Horse & Hound* and it is plain to see that its whiskers have been taken off and the insides of its ears trimmed, you have to wonder if we are going to get to the stage where exhibitors will go so far that there will be a backlash. This has already happened, to a certain extent; in Connemara classes, breed society members and judges have now been told that they are to penalize exhibitors who shorten manes and tails too much and that feather must not be trimmed.

The following section is meant as a guideline, but remember that it's difficult to provide these when you are trying to find your way across a minefield! If in doubt, take a cautious approach and watch lots of classes to see how the riders at the top of the lines present their animals.

Mountain and Moorland

Just to make it even more confusing, whilst pure-bred natives are shown in a (fairly) natural state, part-breds should be pulled, plaited and trimmed. And if you want your pony to compete in, say, ordinary working hunter pony classes as well as mountain and moorland ones, you need to find a compromise but accept that it won't be perfect.

This usually applies only to Welsh and Connemara ponies, which don't have the same amount of hair and feather as their heavier counterparts. You may have to do more plaits than you would ideally like in order to avoid ending up with a row of golf balls along the neck and will either have to plait the tail or give an illusion of a pulled one. The best way of doing this is to apply hair gel – the sort sold for humans and an essential in any show competitors' grooming box – to the top of the tail on the show morning, then apply a tail bandage. If you leave the bandage on until the last possible minute before your class, you will hopefully find the effect lasts long enough.

CONNEMARA

Feather should not be trimmed, nor should you cut a bridlepath at the poll. Manes should not be pulled and thinned so that they look like show ponies, but plenty of brushing or combing will keep them at a manageable thickness, especially if you want to plait for other classes. Tails are usually squared off at the bottom, but left longer than in 'straight' showing classes.

Most people trim under the jaw to give a sharp outline, particularly as Connemaras have quality heads, but you should not trim the inside edges of the ears. However, it seems to be acceptable to trim off the tuft that sticks out at the bottom and becomes dirty and greasy.

Classes for overheight Connemaras have become popular at breed shows. These animals should be turned out in the same way as part-breds, with pulled and plaited manes and pulled or plaited tails. Trimming should be the same as for the nearest equivalent type, e.g. riding horse or hunter.

DALES, FELL AND HIGHLAND

The 'hairy' breeds might not need plaiting, but a mane like this takes a lot of attention

These breeds should be shown without any trimming, though some exhibitors pluck out long hairs under the jaw to give a better idea of an attractive head. Ears should not be trimmed, though you may have the fun of washing tufts that become greasy.

Occasionally, but increasingly rarely, Dales ponies are shown with ribbons in their tails – originally a device to distinguish them from Fells when the two breeds were shown in the same class.

DARTMOOR
Manes and tails should not be trimmed or pulled, but many people like to trim the hair under the jaw to show off these ponies' pretty heads.

EXMOOR
If you show an Exmoor, you will be penalized for any trimming or pulling.

NEW FOREST
New Forest ponies are often shown in the same class as Connemaras and in general, the same turnout rules apply. Manes can be shortened discreetly and tails cut off square.

WELSH
Showing in a natural state takes on a whole new meaning with the Welsh breeds. It's a bit like the philosophy of women wearing natural looking makeup: it can take a lot of skill and time to produce an appearance that is meant to be as nature intended, but with an added gloss! Tails are often thinned at the sides and also pulled lower down so that they end just below the hocks without being squared off. Manes are also thinned and levelled along the bottom edge.

Section A ponies are often shown with one long, thin plait at the top of the mane just behind the ear, to show off the jawline. Jaw hairs are trimmed off and many ponies, particularly the Section As and Bs, are shown with their whiskers trimmed off. Section Cs and Ds are left slightly more natural, but it is becoming increasingly common to see obviously thinned and trimmed manes and tails.

THE JUDGE'S VIEW
I find it worrying that more and more people are trying to make their mountain and moorlands look like show ponies first and natives second. Whilst appreciating that as competition gets stronger and there is an increasingly professional element in

these classes – which is undoubtedly a good thing in terms of improved standards of schooling – we must not lose sight of what these ponies are bred for. They have thick manes and tails with plenty of hair at the top for a reason, to protect them against harsh weather conditions.

My own view, and it's very much a personal one, is that Welsh pony exhibitors in particular are going too far. I don't like seeing ponies who have had their whiskers trimmed off, their manes pulled to four inches long and 'highlighter' round their eyes. They are beautiful enough in their own right and their beauty is intermingled with toughness and soundness.

One of the bonuses of owning a native is that they are so versatile. I appreciate that a lot of owners want to compete in 'ordinary' classes alongside the specialist mountain and moorland ones, particularly in the working hunter pony divisions. Here they are expected to show their ponies with plaited manes and pulled tails, but I'm afraid you have two choices: you either concentrate on M and M classes or accept that your plaits will not be quite as neat as those of some of the other, non-purebred native ponies.

Most judges will accept and sympathize with this and not be too put off by the slight amount of feather on, say, a Connemara, but you certainly won't get much sympathy if you trim up your native and expect to get away with it in breed classes. My attitude now is that if someone comes before me in a mountain and moorland class with what I consider to be an overtrimmed native, I will tell them that I expect to see the pony in a more natural state in future - and that if, later in the season, I am still being presented with a pony that is trimmed to within an inch of its life, I will take this into account when deciding placings.

It might sound harsh, but you should enjoy and accept a native for what it is. Good grooming and very discreet trimming looks far more attractive. Over trimming is, I believe, symptomatic of one of the biggest problems in the native pony world – the breeding and production of ponies with pretty heads, flashy movement and not enough bone or depth of body.

ARABS
Pure-bred Arabs are shown with full, flowing manes and tails. Great emphasis is placed on the beauty of the head; whiskers are left untrimmed but many exhibitors use Vaseline, baby oil or commercial cosmetic preparations to give a gloss around the eyes and muzzles. When overdone, this can look awful, so a light hand is essential.

Pure-bred Arabs are always shown with flowing manes and tails, whilst part-breds and Anglo-Arabs are pulled and plaited

ANGLO-ARABS AND PART-BRED ARABS

Anglos and part-breds are shown with pulled and plaited manes and pulled or plaited tails. As many horses of this breeding are also shown in hack or riding horse classes, the same general rules apply.

COLOURED HORSES

Coloured horses are presented according to the accepted standards of their type. In other words, a hunter will be shown with pulled and plaited mane and pulled tail, a show cob with hogged mane and pulled tail and a traditional with untrimmed, flowing mane and tail. In coloured classes under the auspices of the British Skewbald and Piebald Association or Coloured Horse and Pony Society, follow the rules or guidelines for the appropriate society.

Mainstream classes

After the complications of the above, the rules for hacks, hunters, cobs and riding horses are less confusing. However, it is important to bear in mind the characteristics of each type and to enhance them – so everything about a hack or a show pony should suggest elegance and everything about a cob must give the impression of strength and substance.

HACKS, HUNTERS AND RIDING HORSES

Should be shown with pulled and plaited manes and tails and preferably pulled tails. In theory there is no reason why plaited tails should not be just as acceptable as pulled ones, and in fact they are often seen in in-hand youngstock classes. However, there is still an unspoken rule that if you want to present a professional appearance, your horse should have a pulled tail.

There are all sorts of arguments against this, the main one being that some horses dislike having their tails pulled and may show their objection violently. If your horse comes into this category, you could always use a thinning knife, which is basically a blade inserted into a handle, instead: see later in this chapter for an explanation of various techniques. If you prefer to plait the tail and can do it well, the decision is yours.

These categories should all be trimmed, the aim being to present a sharp outline.

COBS

Cobs are turned out as above, but their manes are hogged. As a plaited tail looks silly with a hogged mane, you have the option of either pulling or 'razoring' the top. Trimming becomes an art form when turning out a cob, especially one with plenty of draught or heavy horse blood. See our before and after pictures for a good example!

RIDDEN SHOW PONIES AND SHOW HUNTER PONIES

Both categories are trimmed, pulled and plaited.

Grooming, strapping and bathing

Opinions vary on the value of grooming in producing a good coat, though it certainly has other benefits: if it's done properly, most horses enjoy the massaging effect and those who appreciate human company like the attention. It also gives you the chance to spot any minor scratches or skin irritations that could otherwise be missed – though good producers can spot an emerging splint or patch of ringworm at 20 paces on a dark night!

Correct feeding is vital to produce healthy skin and coat. The old nagsmen always fed oats to get a shine and the reason this works is that oats have a high oil content. If you prefer not to feed them because they act as a quick release energy source, adding vegetable, corn or soya oil to your horse's diet offers similar benefit in the form of slow release energy.

If you have the time and the elbow grease, grooming should improve the quality of your horse's coat by removing grease. However, this only applies if you keep your grooming brushes and rugs clean. To save on work and washing, try using a cotton summer sheet under your heavier rugs; the cotton sheet is easy and quick to wash and means that you always have a clean layer next to the horse's coat.

Although it has some value in massaging the horse, grooming is mostly done for the sake of appearance. Strapping, on the other hand, can help to build up muscle. Traditionally, this was done with a 'wisp' made from rolled-up and twisted hay or straw, but modern grooms invariably use padded leather strapping pads. The idea is to stimulate the muscles into tensing and relaxing, which is done by applying the strapping pad smartly against the neck or quarters. Start off very gently, or your horse is likely to object violently! You'll find that as he gets used to the process he will tense his muscles in anticipation of the strapping pad landing; most horses enjoy the process and will even lean into the contact. Only strap on the neck and quarters, not on the loins, where you will cause discomfort.

Another essential in most modern producers' grooming kit, even if they don't admit to using it, is spray-on coat gloss. Whilst no one would suggest that it is a good idea to wash out all the natural oils from a coat and try and replace them with a cosmetic preparation from a bottle, gloss and similar de-tangling products are excellent for preventing mane and tail hairs from tangling.

Because they coat the hair, they can also act as a 'stain repellent' and you'll find that shavings can be shaken or brushed out of the tail more easily – a real bonus when you're looking after a native with a full, luxuriant mane and tail. They make the hair slippery, so be careful not to use them in the saddle area or on a mane or tail that is going to be plaited.

The other commonly used cosmetic preparations are hoof oil and gloss, chalk for socks and white markings and highlighters. Keep these solely for use in the ring unless your farrier recommends a product for daily use on your horse's feet; most hoof oils and glosses interfere with the passage of moisture in and out of the hoof so should be kept for ring appearances only. Use a light hand when applying chalk to socks and markings or highlighter. Some people, particularly show pony and Arab exhibitors, go overboard on using highlighter round the eye area with the result that their animals look like shiny-faced pandas.

If you want to disguise a small scar, use one of the 'equine makeup' preparations now sold. The traditional way of getting the same effect is to use appropriately coloured shoe polish and hope that the judge doesn't accidentally come into contact with it!

EXPERT VIEWS

To be honest, our horses don't get groomed that much on a routine basis because we simply don't have the time. Obviously it's important not to put tack or rugs on top of mud, or you'll run the risk of rubs and skin infections, but otherwise I'm a great believer in the philosophy of what you put on the inside being far more effective than what you do to the outside. In other words, feed your horse well and you'll get a good coat.

I have a weakness for greys, which are a nightmare to keep clean. The only way to get rid of stains is to wash them, using a good quality horse shampoo. Some people use washing up liquid, but that's too harsh and will strip the natural oils out of the coat and leave it dull. You can't get a shine on a grey, unless it's an iron grey or dark dapple grey, but if you do the job properly – use an effective shampoo and rinse until the water runs clean – you should be able to get a grey so clean you need to put your sunglasses on!

If you're quick and efficient, then within reason you can bath a horse at any time...though it's asking for trouble to do it on a freezing day when it's blowing a gale, unless you're lucky enough to have indoor facilities. To keep bathing time down to a minimum, get everything ready before you start and if necessary do a kind of strip wash. Do the head, neck and front whilst you've got a rug folded back over the loins and quarters, then fold the rug forwards whilst you do the back end.

We're not lucky enough to have washing boxes and infra-red lamps, so we use the next best thing – thermal rugs which can be put straight on to a wet or sweating horse and 'wick' the moisture through the material, away from the horse.

We're on clay soil, which is a nightmare in winter. Neck covers and hoods can save a lot of work but you must be very careful that there is no risk of a hood slipping when a horse rolls. On the whole, neck covers are safer. Some rugs have built-in neck covers but you need to make sure you don't get a pressure point at the base of the mane. If you do, you might find that a chunk of mane hair falls out, which is the last thing you want.

Hogged manes can be difficult to keep spotless if you have a cob who produces a lot of grease in his coat. Put a bit of white spirit on a barely damp cloth and wipe it over to get rid of the grease.

Lynn Russell

Our horses are groomed every day, but cleaning the grooming kit is as routine as cleaning the horses. When you've finished grooming, add a few drops of surgical spirit to a bucket of water, dip a stable rubber in it and wring it out so it's barely damp and give the horse a final wipe over to remove any remaining specks of dust or grease. You also need to keep your rugs clean.

Some horses, especially Thoroughbreds or those with a lot of Thoroughbred blood, are sensitive and will resent anything but soft brushes. You also have to be careful what you use on manes and tails: metal combs will break the hair.

Kate Moore

We do a lot of strapping, which is a fantastic way to build muscle when done correctly. Once this has been established, it's amazing how they keep it.

Penny Hollings

A JUDGE'S VIEW

A couple of years ago, it seemed as if everyone had gone crazy with highlighters and heaven knows what. Now things have calmed down a bit, thank goodness – though I did hear of one case where someone gave a bay pony a white star by using typewriter correction fluid!

The one thing I do hate to see when I get on a horse is a row of grease specks between each plait or a hogged mane that looks as if it's been snowed on. And whilst I don't mind a bit of Vaseline round the eyes and nostrils on, say, a hack, I don't like the use of cosmetics. I've heard some people advised to use mascara on grey horses' eyelashes, which is ridiculous and could actually cause problems if it gets into the eye. What do they do, take it off with eye makeup remover?

Trimming

Clever trimming can make the world of difference to a horse's appearance – not just the obvious things, such as trimming legs, but little details such as ensuring a neat edge to the hair round the coronet band. It might sound as if it's hardly worth the bother, but you're trying to present a picture in sharp focus, with no blurred edges. The right trimming techniques can also help to make the most of your horse's good points and gloss over any minor imperfections.

You can use clippers or scissors; a clever hand with the clippers gets the best results, but there might be occasions when it's better or safer to use scissors. If so, choose a pair with rounded, not pointed, ends for safety reasons. Electric or battery operated clippers with fine or medium blades will take care of all your trimming tasks, though you might find coarse blades work better when trimming the backs of the legs of some

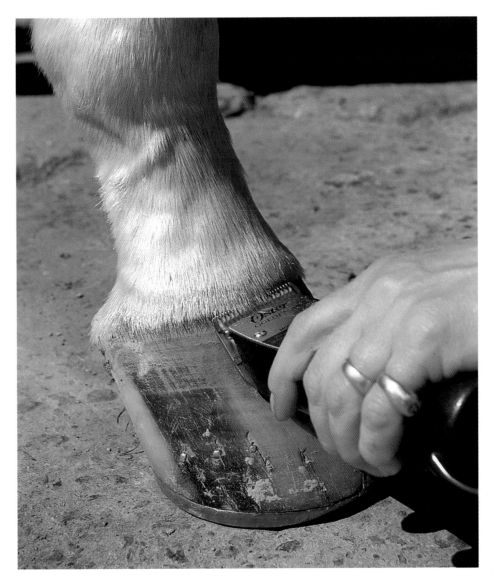

Trimming the hair round the coronet band is one of those finishing touches that makes the final picture

cobs. If you are dealing with a nervous or inexperienced horse, battery operated clippers are usually quieter.

Most horses accept clippers readily on the body as long as you introduce them in a sensible way. Make sure the clippers are well maintained, properly adjusted and lubricated so they don't heat up and that the blades are sharp; blunt blades pull at the coat, which is enough to make any horse object. Before you start clipping, hold your hand against the horse's body and rest the running clippers against it so he gets used to the muted vibration.

Legs are usually easy to deal with unless you get a horse who stamps. This is when you need a helper; if you're clipping a foreleg, get your helper to hold up the opposite foreleg and if you're dealing with a hindleg, ask him or her to hold up the foreleg on the same side.

The head area is the one you're most likely to have problems with until the horse gets used to it, as the vibration passes through the skull. If you're quiet but firm and have plenty of patience, familiarity should eventually breed contempt: until you get to that stage, you might have to use a twitch, as it's too risky to compromise on safety. For the same reason, wear a hard hat and body protector if you're worried about a horse's behaviour – it's better to take precautions than to get injured.

Ignore people who tell you that twitches are cruel. As long as they are applied to the top lip, they do not cause the horse any pain. They work by stimulating the production of endorphins, natural 'feel good' chemicals in the brain that encourage the horse to relax to the extent that some animals will become dozy.

EXPERT VIEW

If I've got a young or nervous horse to clip, I'll tie it up in the barn where we do our clipping and give it a haynet. I can then stand the experienced horses who don't mind clippers next to it and do them first, so the nervous horse realizes that they aren't frightened. This usually gives them so much confidence that they are much easier to deal with when it's their turn.

Kate Moore

The overall picture you are aiming to create is one of smartness and defined edges. Starting at the head, close the horse's ear gently in your hand and run down the edges with a quiet pair of clippers. This gives clean lines but leaves enough protection on the inside against insects and hay seeds. If your horse flatly refuses to let the clippers near his ears, you can get a similar effect by using the same technique and a pair of scissors.

Now check the jawline. If your horse is finely bred, you may not need to do any trimming in this area. If he is slightly thick through the jowl, which is often the case with cobs and some heavyweight hunters, judicious trimming along the underside of the jaw can make the world of difference.

Professionals always trim off their horses' whiskers. Some people believe that this is cruel, their argument being that whiskers are used as feelers, but horses don't seem to miss them. It really is up to you, but if you produce a bewhiskered cob, hack, riding horse, hunter or show pony in the ring you'll lack that final touch.

Most horses look smarter with a small section of mane, usually called a bridlepath, clipped out where the headpiece of the bridle rests. The important thing to remember is that it must be small, or you'll have one fewer plait than would make the perfect picture and will give the optical illusion that your horse is shorter in the neck. If he has a sparse mane and forelock, as can be the case with some Thoroughbreds, don't clip a bridlepath at all – you might need all the help you can get to make a forelock plait.

Be equally cautious about clipping hair at the withers. Before you start, be confident

Neatly trimmed ears help to give a sharp outline

where your first plait will rest and make sure you do not take off any of the hair needed to make this. Again, clipping off too much will make the horse look too short in the neck.

Legs also need to be trimmed down the back and at the fetlock, but be careful not to accentuate any faults. If your horse is fine boned, hold the clippers so that you are clipping with the lie of the coat, not against it, using clippers or scissors to tidy any hair round the fetlocks. If he is a coarser boned cob with hairy heels, clip against the way the coat grows.

Keep chestnuts, the flat, horny growths on the insides of the legs near the knees and hocks, peeled back. If necessary, rub oil or Cornucrescine, a product sold to encourage hoof growth and designed to be massaged into the coronary band, into them to soften them. You may also need to trim the ergots, the horny lumps on the points of the fetlocks, but don't cut them back too far. Either ask your farrier to do it, or use a pair of secateurs.

To give that last, finishing touch, trim the hair round the coronets. Nail scissors work well on fine hair, but to avoid getting a 'pie frill' with thicker, coarser hair it's best to use small clippers, holding them on a slant to get a good finish.

Manes and tails

Pulling and plaiting manes and tails is an art in itself and until you've put in hours of practice, may be enough to make you wish you were showing a mountain and moorland, instead. Cobs at least do not have to be plaited, but there are a few techniques you need to master to keep them looking smart.

Never underestimate the risks – for instance, don't stand behind a horse to pull a tail and if you have to stand on something to pull or plait a mane, remember that you're more vulnerable if the horse decides to throw up its head. Use your common sense and don't expect your horse to be quiet and well behaved if you suddenly decide to pull his mane at the time you normally feed him, or if there is lots going on around him at the time.

PULLING
A nicely pulled mane gives you the basis for a smart set of plaits. To achieve this, you need to have an overall length of four to five inches and an even thickness throughout, so that your plaits are of equal size and shape. This presupposes that your horse has not rubbed a section of mane.

To start pulling, brush or comb the mane through depending on its thickness and the effect you want to achieve. If you're simply trying to thin the mane of a native pony, regular combing may be enough. For proper pulling, try and work when the horse has just been exercised, as the pores of the skin will be more open if he is warm and the hair will come out easier. Some horses don't mind having their manes pulled whilst others are not so keen; in either case, it is kinder to do a little bit at a time rather than attempt the whole job in one go. Many people prefer to use a traditional metal pulling comb, but it's painfully easy to scrape your fingers on the teeth. A strong plastic comb with medium teeth, designed for people rather than horses, can be easier to use. You may also want to put sticking plaster round the joint of your fourth finger, as horsehair cuts skin remarkably easily – and it hurts.

Once you've combed the mane through, you'll usually find that the part along the centre of the neck is the thickest and will therefore need more taking out. The section near the withers is invariably thinner and you may need to shorten it without thinning. Everyone has a preferred way of working, but if you start by thinning the heaviest section, you'll shorten it at the same time. Always pull from underneath: backcomb the top layer out of the way, then take a few strands of hair, wrap them round the comb and pull in an upwards direction. Pulling upwards rather than downwards means the hair comes out more easily and the horse is less likely to object.

Keep combing the mane down and stand back a bit to see the effect you are achieving. Once you've got a reasonably even thickness, you can start evening the length. If you're lucky and your horse has a naturally neat mane, pulling may achieve both aims at once. If you're not, you'll need to nip off the long ends to give an even bottom edge. One way of doing this is to use an old clipper blade: backcomb the top hair and use the blade to take the ends off a very few hairs at a time, then comb down and repeat the process farther along the neck. This gives a neat edge without the blunt ends that scream out that a mane has been scissor cut.

You can get a similar effect by using thinning scissors. Unlike ordinary scissors, these have one ordinary blade and one with teeth, like a small comb. Cut into the hair from underneath, holding the scissors at an angle and taking off the ends of just a few hairs each time. After every few cuts, comb the mane through and move on. This technique can also be used on horses who hate having their manes pulled and are awkward to handle even if you use a twitch. If a horse has tantrums about thinning scissors, then you really have no option but to use a twitch and hope that it will eventually realize that it is making a fuss about nothing.

Pulling tails demands even more caution. If a horse does not like it, he is going to kick, and heaven help you if you are standing in the wrong place at the wrong time: one well-known producer was killed this way, so it is not just a warning for the inexperienced.

The aim in pulling a tail is to enhance the shape of the hindquarters, so you need to

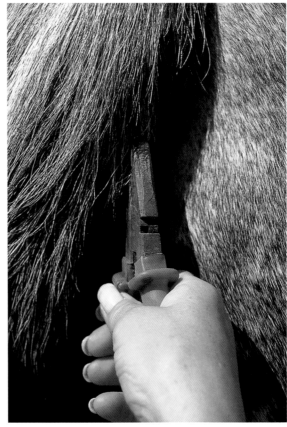

Left: Pulling a tail using a fine-toothed metal comb

Right: Small, square-nosed pliers make pulling short hairs much easier

decide how far down the dock you are going to work. If your horse has slightly weak quarters, you will often get a better effect by not pulling as far down as you would with a horse boasting a powerful back end.

Again, work when your horse is warm after exercise and take out a few hairs at a time. Ideally, you should pull just from the sides, not from the centre, though if you are dealing with a cob that has a thick dock, you may need to take out a small amount of hair from the centre part as well. Be cautious, though, or you will end up with a tail that looks like a loo brush.

Work evenly from both sides and every now and again, check the progress of the effect you are making. If you put a hand under the dock to mimic the natural tail carriage you will get an idea of how it will look from the side when the horse is going and if you stand back, you will see if the tail is keeping an even shape. Once you have pulled a tail, you need to bandage it regularly to help keep the shape; dampen the hair, not the tail bandage.

Although some professionals say that they would never use a razor knife – a

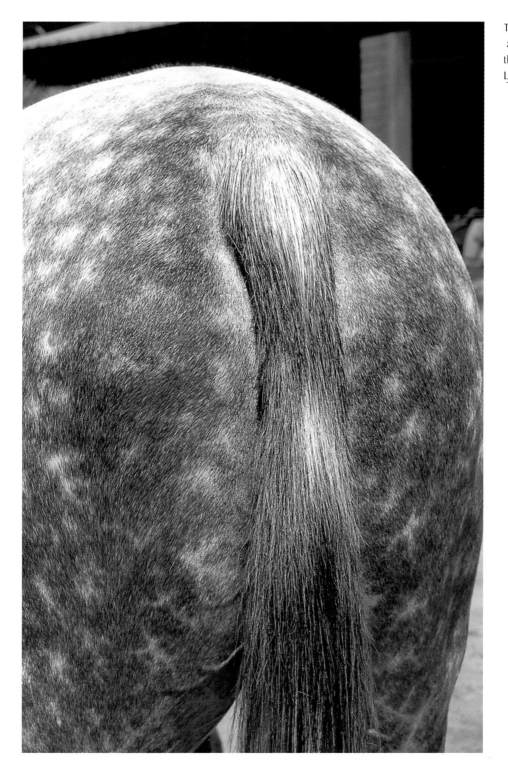

The end result –
a neatly pulled tail
thanks to the skill of
Lynn Russell

If you are at all worried about your horse's reaction to having his tail pulled, stand him in front of bales to deflect any kicks

trimming blade safely enclosed in a plastic case – to try and give the impression of a pulled tail, this may be your only option if a horse or pony objects so violently that to persist is to put yourself in danger. The appearance is not as neat as a well-pulled tail, but is better than getting hurt.

EXPERT VIEW

The most important thing to remember when you're pulling a horse's tail is that you're working in a potentially dangerous area. A lot of people will tell you to pull it over the stable door, but this doesn't make the process any safer – all it means is that you'll be hit by flying chunks of wood when the horse kicks the door out. A much safer way is to build a barrier of straw bales, two small bales high, and stand the horse in front of it. If he kicks, the bales will absorb the blow without hurting you.

It's easier to keep the shape of the tail symmetrical if you work on both sides at the same time. If you have to pull any hair from the centre – which is usually the case with a cob – don't take too much from the top or it will stick out.

Once you've pulled a tail you need to keep it tidied. The easiest way to pull hairs that are too short to hold is to get hold of them with a small pair of square-nosed pliers.

Lynn Russell

The correct – or incorrect – length of tail can make or mar a horse's appearance. Many people show their horses with tails too long and the first thing a judge is going to think is: what is this person trying to cover up? Aim for a finished length of between two and four inches below the point of the hocks when the horse is moving; cobs look better if you aim for the former whilst a hack or riding horse may be better suited by a slightly longer tail. If in doubt, take off half an inch at a time.

To get this right, you need someone to help you. First of all, watch your horse as it is led up in walk and trot to see how high it naturally carries its tail. Then get your helper to put a hand under the dock until the tail is carried at the appropriate height and cut across the bottom. You can use scissors or clippers, but clippers make it easier to cut across in one sweep. Don't try and level tails whilst the horse is simply standing at rest, as it will naturally hold its tail lower – and even if you cut straight across, you will end up with a slanting bottom edge when the horse is moving.

If your horse resents tail pulling to the extent that you cannot do it safely, you will either have to plait it or use a razor comb or thinning scissors on it. Plaited tails look beautiful when done by an expert, but you will not find a professional turning out a horse this way except in in-hand classes. A plaited tail also looks wrong, somehow, on a cob with a hogged mane. If you use a blade or scissors, again work on the sides, not on the

Get a helper to mimic his natural tail carriage before shortening the end with clippers

centre tail hair, and take off a little at a time. Occasionally you see horses whose owners have obviously gone down each side of the dock with clippers, but this never looks right.

PLAITING

At one time, it was frowned on to have anything other than seven or nine plaits, plus one for the forelock. Now, anything goes as long as it suits the horse – though lots of tiny plaits look silly. One tradition that still holds good, though, is that plaits for the show ring should be sewn in, not fastened with rubber bands.

THE EXPERT'S ADVICE

Obviously your horse's mane should be clean, but try and wash it a couple of days before. Squeaky clean hair is slippery and it is harder to keep the plaits tight. You should also try and plait on the day of the show, not the night before, so your plaits don't look 'tired'.

Comb through the mane and divide it into equal sections. Once you've worked out how many plaits suit your horse, cut a plastic comb to the appropriate length and use it as a guide. Some people find it easier to fasten off each section with a rubber band. Before you start plaiting, dampen each section of hair and spray the top with hair gel to help prevent any short hairs at the base of the mane sticking up; remember to shield the other side of the neck with your hand whilst you spray or the coat will get sticky and dull and attract dirt.

Before you go any farther, decide how you need to site the plaits to complement the shape of your horse's neck – or minimize any defects. To emphasize or 'strengthen' a neck that is slightly weak, perhaps because a young horse has not yet muscled up, aim to set the plaits on top of the neck, particularly along the centre section. To slim a thick neck, set them more to the side.

If your horse has a slightly short neck, aim for more plaits rather than fewer ones and take off as little mane hair as possible at the withers. The less common problem – a neck that is so long it looks out of proportion – can be improved by making fewer plaits and taking off slightly more, but not too much, hair at the withers.

To make your plaits sit up on the neck, start plaiting a little way down from the base of the mane hair and keep the plait taut all the way down. Using thread as close as possible to the colour of your horse's mane, pass the needle and knotted thread from the back to the front, then turn over the end of the plait and wrap the thread round. This keeps the loose end hairs under control and helps prevent them sticking out from under the base of your finished plait.

Push the needle through the base of your plait, from back to front, so the plait doubles up. Now roll the plait up to the neck and fasten it with a couple of

A perfectly plaited tail is always smart, but professionals prefer pulled tails

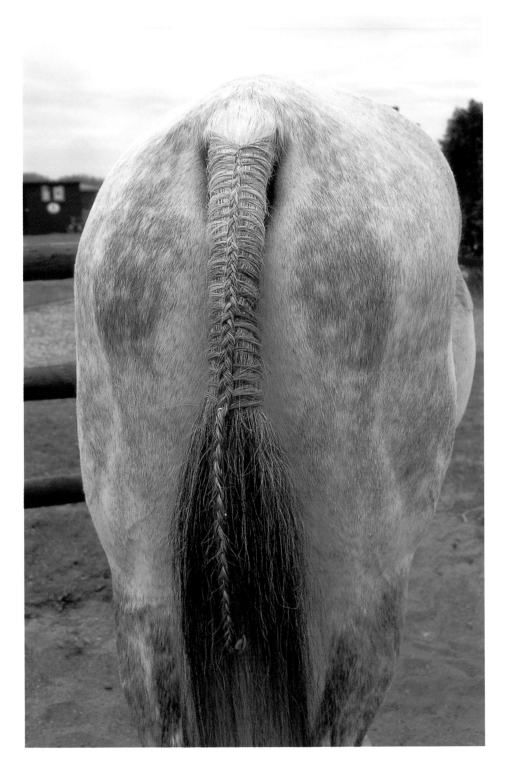

stitches; if you want it to sit on top of the neck, push back as you stitch. If you have plaited the hair tightly enough, there will be no need to wrap thread round the base of the plait and your stitches will be invisible.

If your horse rubs his neck and leaves you with a few straggling hairs where there should be a plait, make a false one! Pull some hair from his tail, or from the mane of a horse of the same colour, and tie the top tightly. Plait down as before and turn over and stitch both ends. Roll up your finished plait and stitch it to the hair that remains – in this situation, you may have to wrap your thread round the loose hair.

Plaiting will not damage the mane hair, but taking out the plaits will if you do not take enough care. Rather than cutting the thread with scissors, use a dressmaker's stitch unpicker so that you can break thread, not hair.

Lynn Russell

PLAITING A TAIL

If you decide to plait your horse's tail, the golden rule is that it must be done to perfection. There are two kinds of tail plait, one where the plait lies flat and the other where it stands out in relief, but in both cases the hair at the dock must be reasonably long. The tail must be clean, or you run the risk of grease specks spoiling the effect, but again it is better to wash it a couple of days before – tail plaits must be kept taut all the way down.

Start by taking a small section of hair from each side of the tail, right at the top. Cross them over and take a third section from the side to the centre of the tail, just below one of the first sections. Plait down the centre of the dock, taking in extra hairs from each side every time you pass the side sections over the centre one. It is important to keep your plaiting tight, so that the 'side bars' stay straight and your plait runs down the centre of the dock, and to only take in a few hairs from the side each time. If you take in too many, your plait will be too thick when you get to the end.

To make a flat plait, use the same technique as for plaiting a mane and pass the side sections over the top of the centre one. For a raised plait, pass them underneath; this may take some practice for those used to plaiting in the conventional way. When you have plaited far enough down to give the right effect – which usually means about two thirds of the way down the dock – finish your centre plait without taking in any more side hairs. Double up the loose ends and secure in the same way as when plaiting a mane, then pass the needle from back to front through the centre of the plait where the side bars finish. You can either leave the end plait loose or stitch it down the centre so that it lies flat, whichever you think looks best.

Don't forget that when you get to the show and take off your horse's tail bandage, you need to unwind it rather than pulling it off to save damaging your plait.

The stages of plaiting a mane. With practice, you might be able to match Lynn Russell's time of under half an hour

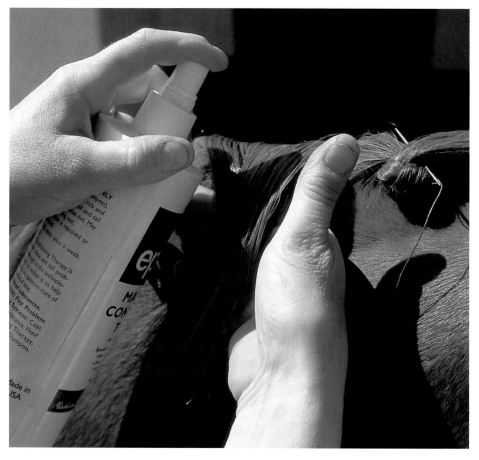

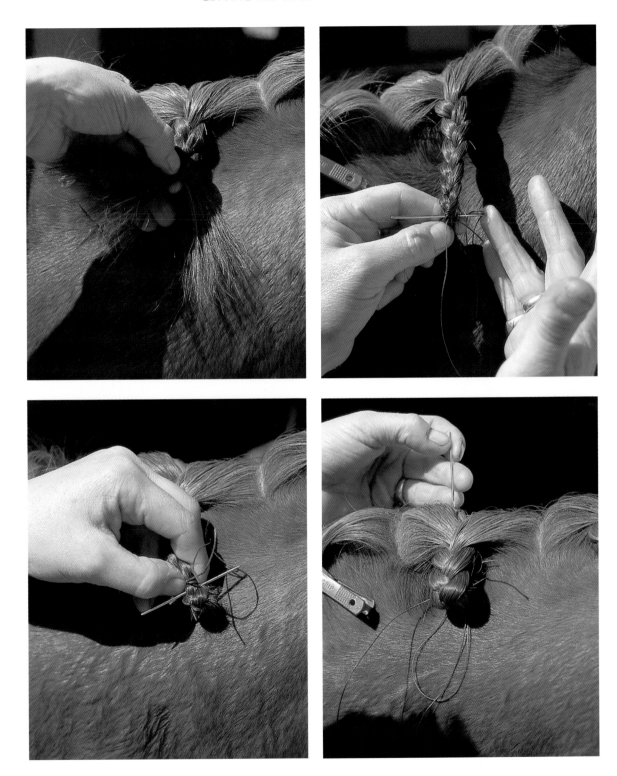

HOGGING A MANE

Cobs are shown with hogged (clipped off) manes to complement their solid, chunky necks. It takes a long time for a hogged mane to grow back, so before you do this, make sure that your horse is a true cob and that he has a reasonably well-muscled neck. A hogged mane won't make a weedy neck look better...just weedier.

The only way to hog a mane is to use clippers, so get your horse used to these first. Again, battery clippers are usually quieter. First clip up each side of the neck, being careful not to cut into the neck hair, then down the centre. With a strong neck, keep the line even, but if you want to bulk out a slightly under muscled neck, leave a little more in the centre of the neck than near the withers and ears. Hogging a few days before the show, to allow a little regrowth, will also give the impression of a stronger neck, but avoid hedgehog impressions.

Greasy hogged manes look as bad as greasy plaited ones. Keep it clean by wiping it with a cloth dampened with witch hazel or surgical spirit.

The three stages of hogging a mane; start by running the clippers down the centre, then each side in turn.

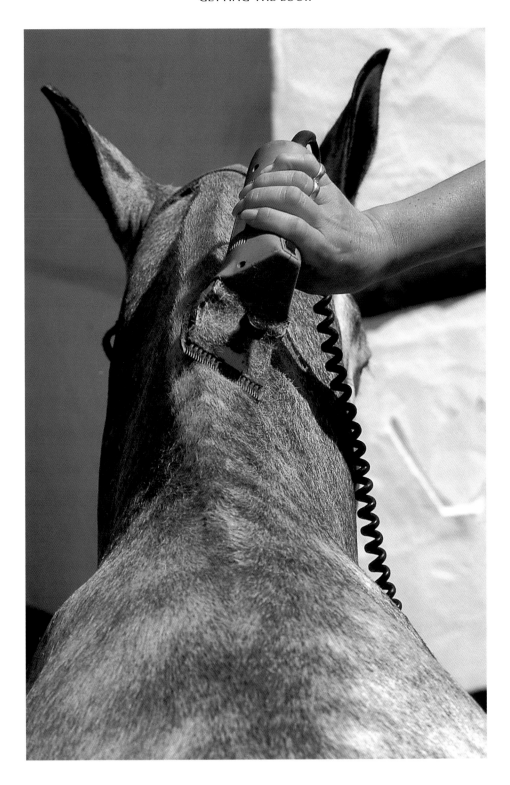

Quarter markings

Quarter markings, designs made by brushing against the lie of the coat, are seen on hacks and riding horses and occasionally on hunters and are nearly always used on show ponies. They are out of place on cobs and never used on mountain and moorlands. Done well, they can add to the horse or pony's elegance; done badly, they catch the judge's eye for all the wrong reasons. If you want to know how best to complement your horse, get an expert to assess him for you and show you what sort of markings to choose and where to place them.

The two main designs are large or small squares or diamonds, giving the effect of a chessboard, stripes and shark's teeth. In all cases, you need a clean, shiny coat to work on and time to apply them before your horse goes in the ring; once you put a rug over them, there is a risk that they will be rubbed off and you will have to start all over again. With practice, though, they take only a couple of minutes to do.

For squares, you can use either a plastic comb cut to an appropriate size or 'cheat' by using a plastic template. The first way is best, as you can tailor the size of the squares to suit your horse, perhaps starting at the top with larger squares and making them smaller as you move down the quarters. The usual method of presentation is to form your squares into either a diamond shape or an inverted triangle, with the 'base' at the top of the quarters.

Small squares are usually used on show ponies and hacks

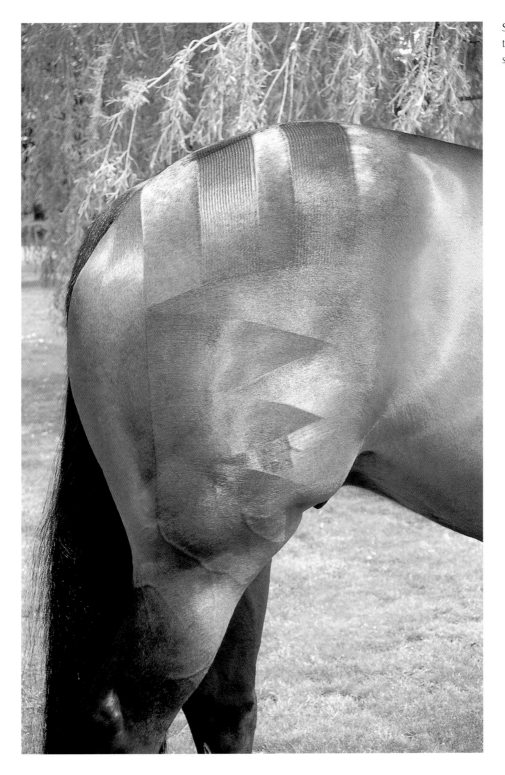

Stripes and sharks'
teeth accentuate
strong hindquarters

Brush the coat thoroughly to remove any traces of dust and grease, then brush over it again with a very slightly damp body brush, following the natural lie of the hair. Using your cut to size comb, comb down rows of squares or diamonds so that they are alternately with or against the lie of the coat. Keep the top row horizontal with the ground rather than following the curve of the quarters.

Shark's teeth are made by preparing the coat in the same way, then using a body brush in broad sweeps, brushing with and against the coat to get the effect you want. Some people like to finish by making a straight edge, holding the body brush vertical and drawing it down from the top of the quarters. Shark's teeth can help to 'fill out' hindquarters that are slightly hollow.

A light coating of hairspray may help to fix the design, especially on a damp day, but keep a light finger on the spray button or you will end up with sticky patches that act as magnets for dust.

Hoof oil

Hoof oil or varnish is the final finishing touch before you go in the ring. You can now buy clear or black products, but in both cases, apply them with a careful hand. Even better, get someone else to put them on for you, especially if you are all dressed up and ready to go. International dressage rider and showing judge Jennie Loriston-Clarke tells the story of the time she organized a display of Britain's native breeds and someone accidentally knocked over a tin of hoof oil near a grey Welsh pony and his rider, turning him into an Appaloosa. Both had to be hastily scrubbed down before they went under the spotlights!

Hoof varnishes may seem more convenient, but if they dry on and have to grow out, they do not do the hooves any good. They may prevent the hoof horn from 'breathing' and thus make it more likely to crack. If in doubt, ask your farrier.

8 TACK AND TOGS

Choosing tack to keep your horse comfortable, show it off to its best advantage and give you and the judge a good ride is an art in itself. The right bridle can change a plain head into a noble one – or make a workmanlike horse look downright ugly – and the right saddle can make the difference between a horse that goes beautifully and gives an armchair ride and one that leaves the judge wanting to get off before he's done half a circuit of a ring. Bits, too, are a potential minefield: in most cases, you will be using a double or a pelham, but how do you work out the right combination of mouthpiece and cheekpiece to suit your horse?

Bridles and bits

Starting from the front end, your bridle should complement your horse's head. The golden rule is that the more workmanlike the head, the more workmanlike the bridle, so a cob needs a bridle with a broader noseband and browband than would suit a riding horse and an elegant hack is suited by narrower leather than you would expect to see on a hunter.

Show ponies' attractive heads are set off best by bridles made from narrow – but not flimsy – leather with stitched nosebands and coloured browbands. The more workmanlike show hunter and working hunter ponies are shown in more workmanlike bridles, with flat nosebands and plain leather, flat browbands. Native ponies should be bridled according to their conformation, so the small, pretty head of a Welsh Section A can take a lighter weight of leather whilst a Dales or Fell needs a substantial bridle to match.

If in doubt, think workmanlike. One of the commonest mistakes seen in the show ring is riders who choose flimsy bridles in the hope that this will give their horse or pony's head more quality. In fact, the opposite applies. It is always worth buying the

A plain bridle with broad noseband and browband complements a cob's workmanlike head.

Bridles of a lighter weight suit the finely built show pony

best quality you can afford – the ultimate is a made to measure bridle that can be adjusted so that the buckles are in exactly the right place.

If you are showing a novice horse, you have the option of using a snaffle bridle; you may also choose to use a snaffle for working hunter classes, depending on what bit your horse jumps best in. In some pony classes, such as lead rein, first ridden and novices, simple snaffle bridles are compulsory under most societies' rules, though Ponies Association (UK) permits 'any suitable bridle' for first riddens, preferring to leave the choice to exhibitors. However, most judges would look askance at anything other than a snaffle in this category.

For cob, hunter, riding horse and hack classes, most competitors prefer to go straight into pelhams or doubles and as you will see later in this chapter, these are

A riding horse equipped in a bridle with coloured browband and Rugby pelham

inevitably the professionals' choice. Double and pelham bridles are always used with two reins and the top (bradoon or snaffle) rein should be wider than the bottom (curb) one. The weight must be appropriate for the type of horse, but as a rough guideline, go for five eighths or three quarters of an inch wide leather for the top rein and half an inch for the bottom one. 'Shoestring' reins that are too thin are not as safe and most judges hate them.

It is down to individual choice – and perhaps how well you can hold your horse in the gallop – as to whether you use plain leather reins or prefer extra grip on the top pair. Plaited or laced bradoon reins are effective and smart, especially in wet weather; some riders like reins designed originally for dressage, with a rubber grip on the inside and plain leather on the outside to give grip but traditional appearance. Curb reins should always be plain leather.

No one will send you out of the ring in disgrace for using the 'wrong' bridle, but to avoid sticking out like a sore thumb, these are the accepted standards. Tradition dictates that tack for the show ring should always be brown, not black, though some exhibitors showing in coloured horse classes believe that black tack looks better on a piebald:

Hunters and cobs – workmanlike bridles with broad, plain, flat nosebands and browbands. Coloured or brass clencher browbands are never used on these horses.

Working hunters and working cobs – follow the basic guidelines above, but if necessary, you can substitute a noseband which gives more control for the standard cavesson style.

Hacks – finer, but not flimsy, leather. Nosebands and browbands may be padded and stitched. Coloured browbands covered in velvet ribbon are universal.

Riding horses – more substantial than many hack bridles, with plain or coloured browbands. Nosebands and plain browbands can be flat or padded and stitched. The final choice depends on what best suits your horse's head, but if in doubt, tend towards hunterweight bridles rather than hack ones.

Arabs – flimsy shoestring bridles made from rolled leather are, thankfully, not seen as often as they used to be. The top riders, who prove that a well-made, correctly schooled Arabian can go as well as any other breed or type, favour hack-type bridles with plain coloured browbands and their horses' beautiful heads need no farther adornment.

Mountain and moorland – think workmanlike but complementary. Some exhibitors and judges do not seem to mind brass browbands on, say, ridden Connemaras, whilst others stick with the view that these are out of place on anything other than driving animals.

Coloured horses – choose a bridle which is appropriate for your horse or pony's type, e.g. hunter, cob, mountain and moorland.

Show ponies – narrower leather, with stitched nosebands and coloured browbands covered in velvet ribbon.

Show hunter ponies – broader leather with plain, flat nosebands and browbands.

Working hunter ponies – follow the same guidelines as for show hunter ponies. As with working hunters, you can substitute a noseband which gives more control if necessary and use a martingale.

EXPERT VIEW

The commonest mistake amateurs make is to use bridles that are too lightweight. The weight of a bridle is defined by the width of the cheekpiece, with everything else made in proportion. The classic measurements are that a hunter bridle has three quarters of an inch cheekpieces, which means the noseband will be about two inches wide; hack bridles have half inch cheekpieces and riding horse ones can be hunter weight or slightly less, depending on the type of head.

I like nosebands that are stitched to the cheekpieces rather than the slotted kind, as they lie flat to the head. In straight showing classes you should only use cavesson nosebands; there's nothing to stop you using a Flash or Grakle in a workers' class, though I always think that if a horse jumps and rides well in a double or pelham bridle, it looks better. It is, after all, a showing class rather than a show jumping one.

If your horse tends to try and open his mouth, a broad cavesson noseband dropped down a hole and fastened a bit tighter than usual can do the trick. So can a doubleback or cinch noseband, where the back strap goes through a metal loop and doubles back on itself to fasten. Some people still call this the Grandstand noseband, because Keith Luxford, the saddler, brought one out for his cob, Grandstand.

Remember that you're showing your horse, not showing off his tack. Keep it discreet, even when you're using a coloured browband on a hack or a riding horse. With these, choose two or three colours that 'lift' the horse's head. Personally, I hate coloured browbands with flapping ornaments at each end – the only rosettes I want to see on a bridle are the ones that I win!

It pays to buy the best you can afford and if you're going to show regularly, to have a bridle that you keep purely for showing. Use a cheaper work bridle for everyday and your show bridle will stay smarter for longer. New leather needs suppling up – a judge won't thank you if he gets on your horse and the reins won't bend. Whenever we get new reins, we hang them up in the tack room for a few days and regularly work in a mixture of oil and saddle soap. If you knead this in with your fingers every time you walk past, they soon become softer.

Traditionally, the very best show bridles are handmade and have 14 stitches to the inch. They don't come cheap, so if you're on a tighter budget, there's nothing wrong with machine stitched tack as long as the leather is good quality. Cheekpieces and reins have stud billets rather than buckles to give a neater look; traditionally, bits were stitched in, but this means you can't swap bits from one bridle to another.

I prefer plain leather reins, though a lot of riders like a laced or plaited top rein. Rubber grip reins are unattractive and too bulky and even the ones with a rubber grip down the inside can leave rub marks on a fine coat.

Whatever sort of bridle you use, make sure it fits properly. It's amazing how many people use ill-fitting tack and this affects the way the horse goes as well as its appearance. A browband that is too short will pinch the base of the ears and one that is too long will sag and flap around. The noseband should come below the base of the facial bones, but not too low. Sometimes, it's amazing what a difference you can make to the appearance of a horse's head just by altering the height of the noseband.

Ideally, the buckles of the cheekpiece, noseband and throatlatch should be level with the horse's eye, in a neat row. This is where a made to measure bridle is so lovely, as you can get everything exactly right.

Lynn Russell

A JUDGE'S VIEW

I can't stand reins that are so thin it's like holding a pair of shoelaces. Competitors in the Arab classes are the worst offenders and they don't seem to realize how potentially dangerous this is.

In some classes, people try too hard to stand out. You see this in mountain and moorland classes – I know that if you've got a grey Connemara in a class of twenty other grey Connemaras it must be tempting to try and catch the judge's eye, but I do wish that people would remember that a good animal will always stand out on its own merit and a sparkly browband or bright yellow breeches might dazzle the judge, but not in the way they hope for!

The unwritten rule is that horse exhibitors and those with ponies in open classes should use a bridle with double reins – a pelham or a double. There are so many types of pelham and so many permutations on mouthpieces and cheekpieces in double bridles that a lot of people get totally confused. If this sounds familiar, your best bet is

A collection of pelhams from Lynn Russell's tack room

to find a successful professional producer who will assess you and your horse and make suggestions; professionals usually have well-stocked tack rooms and as long as you accept that you have to treat this as a service that has to be paid for, will try different bits to find something your horse is happy with.

Although many people have strong views on the subject, there is nothing written in stone to say that a double bridle is better than a pelham or vice versa. In the right hands, a correctly fitted double bridle allows perhaps the ultimate in refined communi-

143

The Belton bit,
brought out recently

cation. On the other hand, there are some horses who are not comfortable in two bits but are much happier in pelhams. As its detractors are quick to point out, a pelham is less precise in its action because it tries to combine two actions in one mouthpiece – but a lot of horses don't seem at all bothered by this!

Interestingly, a new bit – or at least, a new combination of mouthpiece and cheekpiece backed up by a lot of knowledge – is designed to be used either in its own right or as an introduction to a double bridle. The Belton bit, with loose rings, revolving cheeks and a mouthpiece with a tongue groove, was designed by Paul Belton, the chairman of Albion Saddlemakers and is already proving popular.

If you have to go it alone, the guidelines in this section should help. Before you start, check that your horse's mouth and teeth are in good condition – which means calling in a horse vet with a recognition of the importance of dentistry or a qualified dental technician. You also need to look at the mouth conformation, something an amazing number of people appear not to bother with.

For instance, if your horse has a fat, fleshy tongue he will probably be uncomfortable in a bit with a thick mouthpiece, because he simply won't have room for it in his mouth. Whilst a thick mouthpiece is theoretically milder than a thinner one, in practical terms this does not always hold true. Similarly, a horse of this kind may go much more happily in a bit with a port (central arch) than a straight bar mouthpiece.

If he has a tiny mouth and a short jaw, you will nearly always get better results using a pelham than a double bridle – again, because the horse does not have enough room in his mouth to take two bits. The correctly chosen and fitted double bridle is a wonderful instrument in the right hands and would nearly always be the first choice for a hunter, but the advantage of showing is that – unlike dressage – a pelham is just as acceptable.

Bits are now made from a wide range of metals, including compositions designed to encourage a horse to salivate and mouthpieces covered in special 'plastics'. This, too, gives lots of scope for solving problems. However, you have to remember that plastic and rubber covered bits do not stand up to horses' teeth and that you need to be absolutely sure that there is a safe, central metal core so that if the horse chews right through the coating, you are not suddenly left with no bit and no control.

The type of curb chain you use can make a big difference, especially to a sensitive horse. Most horses go well with a double link stainless steel one, but light mouthed horses often prefer curb chains where the part which goes under the jaw is made from leather or elastic. It is always correct to use a leather lipstrap, which helps to make sure that the curb chain sits in the right place on the jaw – and means you are less likely to lose it when carrying bridles around! At one time, lipstraps were universal, but for some reason many people no longer bother with them.

Although it may seem an obvious thing to state, bits must be the right size and properly adjusted. Unfortunately, you only have to walk round any show ring to see plenty examples of how not to do it: the commonest fault is to use a bit with a mouthpiece that is too big. If this is compounded by adjusting it so that it hangs slightly too low, you get even more problems – the bit will often bang against a gelding's tushes and the horse may be tempted to try and get his tongue over it.

A correctly adjusted bit will fit snugly into the corner of the horse's mouth, without making him look as if he is smiling. However, if he has fleshy lips, you may need to adjust it a hole higher than initially seems correct – open his mouth and see where the mouthpiece lies. If it is the right size, you should not be able to fit more than the width of an adult's little finger between the bit ring and the corner of the mouth on each side. If the bit has a jointed mouthpiece, straighten it in the mouth by putting a thumb in each ring and exerting gentle pressure before trying this test.

Finding the right bit for your horse is essential whatever job he is meant to do but it is only part of the story. If a horse is resistant or unhappy in his mouth, the underlying cause may be nothing to do with the choice of bit or even the state of his teeth – it could be down to a sore back, resistance because he does not understand what you are asking him to do or because you are pushing him too hard, too soon or simply that you are a rider with bad hands. But if you keep that in mind, the following suggestions may help.

The horse who leans on the bit, and/or is dry or 'dead' in the mouth will usually go better in bits which allow maximum play. This includes double bridles with loose ring bradoons and sliding cheek curbs, Rugby pelhams – which have a loose ring set outside the cheek – and the SM pelham. Materials which encourage salivation include sweet iron and metals with a high copper content such as Kangaroo and Aurigan.

Horses with the opposite problem, who tend to come behind the bit and lack confidence in taking a contact, are usually better suited by bits which naturally stay more stable in the mouth. This includes eggbutt bradoons, fixed curbs and mullen mouth pelhams. If the action of the curb chain is a problem, try one made primarily from elastic or leather.

Lead rein and first ridden ponies are nearly always shown in snaffle bridles, usually a simple eggbutt, though there has been some controversy over one organization's rule that 'any suitable bridle' may be used. Some exhibitors looked on this as approval to produce first ridden ponies in double bridles, which has not met with wide approval. With lead rein ponies, it is important to remember that the leather lead rein must always be attached to the noseband, not to the bit. This means that couplings used for in-hand showing which attach to the bit and the noseband or simply to the bit rings are not permitted.

There is such a huge variety of snaffles that it should be reasonably easy to find one to suit your novice or first ridden pony. Fashions come and go, but the standard eggbutt and loose ring snaffles remain tried and tested. Small mouths cannot take bulky mouthpieces and small heads are complemented by small bit rings.

A lot of small children find it difficult to keep their hands still when they rise to the trot, because they do not have the length of leg to give them a stable seat. You can then get a vicious circle, with ponies tossing their heads or trying to go faster to avoid discomfort and their riders becoming even more unbalanced. Pete Wilkinson, a saddler and successful show pony producer and judge, developed the Wilkie snaffle to try and overcome these problems and it has certainly caught on in the showing world.

The Wilkie snaffle comprises a loose ring with two smaller ones, one set outside the main ring to take the bridle cheekpieces and the other inside to take the reins. It can be bought in a variety of mouthpieces, including single jointed and French link, and is now accepted by most judges. Poll pressure asks the pony to lower its head and the slight movement of the main rings stops the mouthpiece being 'dead' in the mouth. Whatever the theory behind a bit, the proof is in the horse or pony's reaction to it, and a lot of animals seem to like it.

Open ponies are ridden in pelhams or double bridles; as with horses, both are equally correct. They should be used with double reins, though on rare occasions you

Two versions of the Wilkie snaffle, particularly popular with pony producers

see smaller children using split reins on a pelham bridle. These are joined halfway between the mouthpiece and centre buckle on each side so the child only has one rein in each hand. Ordinary pelham couplings or D-rings are never used. If you use a pelham but want the pony's head to have a more 'finished' look, then use a sliphead fastened to the top ring.

You occasionally see show ponies ridden in Globe pelhams, which are actually misnamed. This bit is a small curb and as it is used with one rein obviously does not have the finesse of a pelham with two reins or a double bridle.

EXPERT VIEWS
I look more at the horse's way of going than its age when deciding if it is ready to go into a double bridle or pelham. It must first be going well in a snaffle, going forwards properly, accepting the bit and engaging behind. I do feel very strongly that basic schooling should be the same whatever the horse's eventual job is going to be. It might go off to be a dressage horse, show jumper, show horse or whatever, but the basics must be the same – it must go freely forwards and straight.

Once the horse is established, I would tend to work it in a snaffle at home and only use a double bridle at shows. There are so many types and variations that it is important to look at the conformation of a horse's mouth and jaw before making a decision.

I always look at the length of the jaw, because some horses, especially Thoroughbreds and ponies, have tiny mouths and it can be difficult to fit a double. You also need to look at how low the molars are and that with a gelding, the tushes are in the 'right' place. Some horses have large, fleshy tongues, and in that case, I would often choose an arched mouth Weymouth (curb) or one with a higher port to provide more room for the tongue.

You also have to decide on the appropriate length and type of the cheekpieces. The horse who is naturally light or tends to come behind the bit would often be happier with a fixed cheek, whilst a sliding one can be better for the horse who tends to lean. Similarly, I will often choose a loose ring bradoon for a horse who needs more 'play' in the mouthpiece and an eggbutt one if it responds better to a mouthpiece which stays relatively still.

The length of the curb cheekpieces affects the potential leverage. When you arrive to judge and see something in the ring with a six-inch cheekpiece, you wonder what it's going to do! I always say that a horse is only as good as its rider, but if you have one that gets into the ring and says 'I'm galloping whether you like it or not' it can be better to put it in a slightly sharper bit, which it respects, than to hang on in a theoretically milder one.

The standard measurement for cheekpieces, with Weymouths and pelhams, is that the overall length of the cheekpiece is the same as the width of the mouthpiece. There are also bits with relatively smaller cheekpieces, often called Tom Thumbs, which are particularly useful for animals with small mouths.

When you fit a double bridle, the bradoon should sit snugly into the corners of the mouth without pulling up the lips. With the Weymouth, the old saying was that it should be one inch above the tushes in a gelding and two inches above the corner teeth in a mare. Precise adjustment depends on the length of the horse's jaw, but these guidelines are still useful.

I like the curb chain to come into play when the curb cheekpiece is drawn back to an angle of 45 degrees. It is a mistake to have it too loose: you sometimes see cases where the Weymouth comes right round to 180 degrees. When the curb chain is fitted correctly, you can ride on a very light curb rein. What you want to achieve by using the curb rein is for the horse to flex and relax its jaw.

Richard Ramsay, producer and judge

I'm a great fan of French link snaffles, which have a kidney-shaped central link and are more comfortable for most horses than the ordinary single-jointed snaffle, and a French link pelham is equally useful. It can be an ideal stepping stone – we often use a French link snaffle to start off a young horse and the pelham with this mouthpiece can be perfect if it is not ready to go straight into a double bridle.

I have one very useful pelham which has a French link mouthpiece and Rugby cheeks. The loose rings of the Rugby pelham are outside the cheekpieces, so there is no danger of the horse's mouth being pinched.

Kate Moore

A lot of ponies come to me for breaking and initial schooling before starting their showing careers. I tend to keep it simple and start off with an eggbutt snaffle, but if the pony doesn't seem happy with this would switch to something else, often a French link.

I always use a standing martingale to start with, which I know is very unfashionable these days, but it works for me! The nose is the first point of control for any young horse or pony when it is led and this seems to follow through in a logical fashion. Some people say that because a standing martingale attaches to the noseband, it encourages the horse to set itself against it, but I don't find that this happens – perhaps because I don't let young ponies set themselves against me when they are being led. The good thing about a standing martingale is that it has no influence on the reins, so can't interfere with the mouth.

Once the pony is working nicely in a snaffle, without a martingale, I often switch to a pelham with the same type of mouthpiece – so if it has been happy in an ordinary jointed snaffle, I'll use a little jointed pelham. This again seems to be logical, as if you ride mainly off the top rein there is very little difference, but you can use a little curb rein if you need to.

Julia Woods

I get very annoyed when people make out that the snaffle is always milder than the pelham. In the wrong hands, the snaffle can be very harsh and in the right hands, the pelham is a bit that most horses much prefer. When we back young show horses, we use a snaffle for the first few weeks but then put them straight into a pelham. They learn to carry themselves much more easily and quickly, which means that horse and rider both stay happy.

A pelham is correct for all showing classes and the majority of horses go better in a straight bar or mullen (half-moon) mouthpiece than a single jointed one. There is one simple reason why many horses are so much easier to ride in a pelham than a snaffle – they are more comfortable and so less resistant.

The SM and Hanoverian pelhams are perhaps less well known than other versions, but they are very useful in the fight hands. The SM has hinged sides, which give independent rein action, and a mouthpiece which allows enough room for the tongue and stays at the correct angle in the mouth however the horse holds its head. The Hanoverian pelham has a roller set into the mouthpiece, which discourages horses from rolling their tongues up and back. Young horses often seem to like it.

I know a lot of people say that a pelham bridle never looks as 'finished' as a double, but there is an easy way to rectify this – attach a sliphead from a double bridle to the top ring. This is especially effective with a Rugby pelham, because of the separate loose ring.

Lynn Russell

I don't like stainless steel bits, I much prefer Happy Mouth or Kangaroo metal ones because they encourage more play in the mouth. For the same reason, I prefer jointed pelhams to straight ones - a lot of ponies like a jointed Kangaroo pelham.

Another bit that can be useful for corrective purposes is the Wilkie snaffle, which has a large ring with two small ones. The bottom one is inside the main ring and the top one set outside it, so you get a bit of poll pressure in a mild acting way. We found it very useful for a pony which 'locked' on one side.

Penny Hollings

Saddles

The first consideration when choosing a show saddle, as with any other kind, is that it should fit the horse. It must also suit the rider, because an uncomfortable or unbalanced rider – and the two will inevitably go together – will put stress on the horse, leading to discomfort, pain and damage.

With a show saddle, there is even more to think about, because your tack is part of your horse's overall appearance and should enhance his conformation. It also needs to be suitable for a judge to ride in who may not be the same size and shape as you.

Your saddle should look as if it follows the lines of the horse, so needs to sit well on the back rather than be perched on top. This means that the tree – the frame on which the saddle is made – should follow the profile of the back, which is one of the first rules of saddle fitting under any circumstances. It should have broad panels to spread the rider's weight over as large an area as possible and sufficient, but not excessive, clearance under the pommel and cantle.

Whatever type of horse or pony you are riding, whether it is a show hack or a mountain and moorland pony, your saddle should be reasonably straight cut in order to show off its shoulder. Occasionally you see exhibitors riding in dressage saddles, but most are not suitable for the show ring. Dressage is a different discipline that requires a straighter leg position and a lot of judges will not be happy riding on a dressage saddle; you certainly would not be very comfortable or secure galloping a big, onward bound hunter in one. You would also have to use a short dressage girth, which covers up the elbow area and looks out of place. Having said that, there are a few styles – especially older designs – which are not quite as straight cut and could be adapted to take a standard girth. These are likely to be only available secondhand and most showing riders who own them would not part with them for any price.

As showing has become more and more popular, so saddles have been designed specifically for this discipline. Some, particularly those developed with professional showing riders, have proved very successful. They have very discreet knee and perhaps thigh rolls that give a little support and stability, coupled with flattish seats. Some

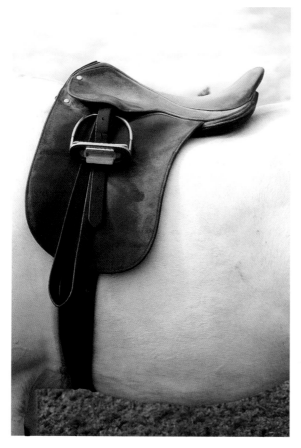 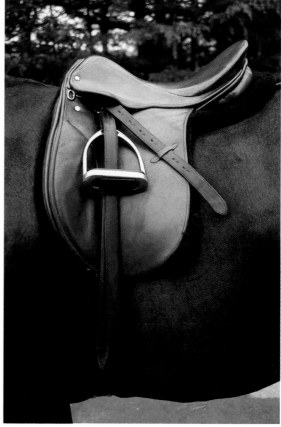

Two show saddles designed to show off the horse's shoulder

Another show
saddle designed to
show off the
horse's shoulder

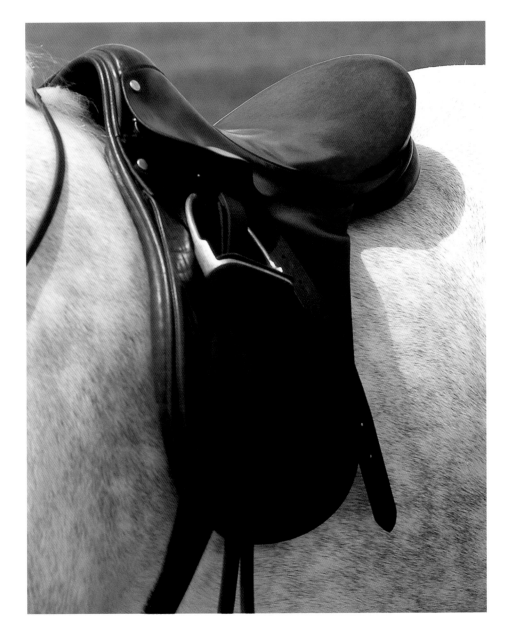

professional riders prefer to use saddles without knee or thigh rolls because they look
so good: these are often made from reversed hide (suede) to give better grip.

At the end of the day, it comes down to what you ride best on. This applies particularly
to working classes, where no change of tack is allowed between the jumping and showing
phases. Whilst it is best not to use a saddle that is too forward cut and covers up the
shoulder, you don't want to fall off your aesthetically perfect show saddle in mid-air.

Saddles, like bridles, are traditionally made from brown leather for the show ring. Again, you may see competitors showing true piebalds – horses without any brown hairs in their coats – in coloured classes who feel that black looks better against a black and white coat.

Some types of animal are harder to fit than others. Cobs and large mountain and moorland breeds can be quite a challenge, particularly if they have no withers to speak of coupled with broad, flat backs. It can be like trying to fit a saddle to a barrel and you need a really good saddle fitter, preferably someone who can do any necessary adjustments directly. There are lots of ways to help, but it often takes an expert eye and a lot of experience to get the best results. Remember, too, that horses and ponies change shape as they gain or lose weight and muscle up through schooling and work, so don't assume that a saddle which fits your four-year-old or fat horse now will fit him in a few months. Don't begrudge money spent on regular checks and, where necessary, adjustments if you want your horse to work to his best ability.

If you are particularly small, your show saddle should still be large enough in the seat to accommodate judges of more ample proportions. Similarly, stirrup irons should be big enough to be safe for riders with larger feet and leathers must be sized to adjust up or down enough to suit long or short-legged judges.

Girths should be made from leather and be the same colour as your saddle, unless

This saddle, used by Kate Moore in working hunter classes, is more forward cut to allow a comfortable jumping position but does not detract from the horse's conformation

you are showing a grey or coloured horse with a white belly area. In these cases, white webbing or lampwick girths often look better, because they do not visually cut the horse in two. The disadvantage is that they are a pain to keep clean and you will have to keep them just for the show ring.

If your horse is comfortable without a numnah, don't use one: a well-fitting saddle alone looks neater and smarter. However, if your horse or pony is sensitive, you are better off using a discreet numnah or gel pad. Choose one the same colour as your saddle, of a style that shows as little as possible. Some companies sell made to measure brown sheepskin numnahs that protrude no more than half an inch round the edges of your saddle and whilst they are more expensive than standard ones, the improved appearance they offer makes them well worth the extra. Nothing looks worse than a pie frill round your saddle!

Try a couple of tips from Lynn Russell. If you soap the underneath of your saddle and do not wipe off the excess, a sheepskin that has been cut to fit will not slip. You can also use a dampened chamois leather, again cut to fit so that it does not show round the edges.

EXPERT VIEWS

There are basic fitting guidelines that apply whatever sort of animal you're dealing with, but some circumstances present particular headaches. Cobs and large native breeds can be a challenge sometimes. I've never been defeated, but I've had some where I've had to use every answer I know!

With a show cob, especially one that's too fat, you often have no withers, a back like a table top and a round barrel. The good thing is that as cobs have become so popular, more saddle makers are addressing the problem and it's easier to find saddles that have the correct tree profile.

The commonest problems with natives are that they are either completely flat backed, which tends to go with natural rotundity, or they tend to have dipped backs. For instance, Welsh breeds often have very slight sway backs: it doesn't mean that they are weak, it's just a conformation characteristic.

Because the large breeds are so strong, a lot of adults ride them. Fitting a saddle can be difficult when you have a broad-in-the-beam rider on a short-backed pony, as you can't have pressure on the pony's loins.

I still find that a lot of riders put their saddles too far forwards, so that as the top of the shoulder rotates back, the horse's movement is impeded. Occasionally, I get people who call me out because they're worried that their saddle is slipping back, when in fact they're putting it on too far forwards and it's actually settling into the right place!

If a saddle slips, fitting a point strap – an extra girth strap attached to the points of the tree – can help in some cases. There is also a design of numnah called the Impakt which may help, which comes in discreet colours and can be cut to fit.

Malan Goddard, Master Saddler

I prefer suede saddles to leather ones because they enable the rider to feel more secure. It's no good having a saddle that looks wonderful on the pony if the child doesn't feel safe. The straighter cut saddles are best for show and show hunter ponies as they show off the shoulder and help the rider to sit correctly, but don't use one with a high pommel and cantle or it will make your pony look longer in the back. For working hunter ponies, a general purpose saddle is best.

Penny Hollings

If you aim to show your horse in classes for ladies' hunters suitable to be ridden side-saddle, the side-saddle itself will make a hefty dent in your bank balance. Making side-saddles is a dying art and most professionals say that the old saddles – made by names such as Owen, Champion and Wilton, Mayhew and Whippy – are worth their weight in gold.

Fitting them is also a specialist job and your best bet, as with all things sideways, is to contact the Side Saddle Association. They keep lists of saddlers and instructors and may also have details of members who have saddles for sale.

EXPERT VIEW

As a rider and a judge, I know that if a side-saddle does not fit a horse it can do a lot of damage – and if it's uncomfortable to ride on, it doesn't give a good impression. Side-saddles are heavier than ordinary ones and in the golden days of side-saddle riding they were not only made to measure for individual clients but constructed so that ladies who rode every day could alternate between riding on the nearside and the offside. It was believed that this helped prevent curvature of the rider's spine but probably did even more for the horses' backs.

A side-saddle is different in lots of ways from an ordinary one. Instead of the tree fitting across the withers and being equally adjusted on either side, it is longer on the nearside than the offside. You're therefore starting from scratch with something unbalanced – and adding two pommels on the nearside to unbalance it even more.

There are three straps to keep it in place, an ordinary girth, a balance girth or strap and a safety girth. The balance strap is designed to keep the balance of the

It is important that
side-saddles are
fitted by an expert

saddle equal on the horse's back. It doesn't take much imagination to realize that it feels very different for the horse who is only used to an astride saddle – some are bothered by the feel of the balance strap to start with.

It's important not to assume that you can just plonk on a side-saddle and ride off into the sunset. Most horses accept it readily, but for safety's sake you must introduce it carefully. Put the saddle on, then do the balance strap up just tight enough to keep everything in place. Lead the horse forwards and walk him round on both reins until he gets used to the feel of it, then tighten it gradually.

Lynn Russell

Training aids

Training aids - or gadgets, depending on your point of view – can never be a substitute for correct schooling, but do have their place. Because they are used to develop or improve a horse or pony's way of going, they are dealt with in the next chapter.

Tack care

Cleaning tack is a rotten job, but someone has to do it – and if you've spent a lot of money on quality leatherwork, you shouldn't begrudge it. One way of making sure that your lovely showing bridle stays pristine is to get it in a nice supple condition then save it for the show ring, using an old work bridle or synthetic design for everyday. The best synthetics no longer look cheap and nasty and can be machine washed.

Synthetic saddles have also improved, but must be fitted with as much care and expertise as expensive leather ones. Don't make the mistake of thinking that because they are lightweight, they can't do any damage. And if you get used to riding in a synthetic saddle, have a few practice rides on your leather one before the start of the season to reacquaint yourself with its different feel.

EXPERT VIEW
Life is too short to spend hours every day cleaning tack but as your and your horse's safety depends on it being in good condition, it is important to look after it. Safety checks take only minutes: always give tack a quick look over as you're getting ready, whether it's your own horse or someone else's.

Once a week, check vulnerable areas such as stitching and anywhere that metal rests on leather. Get hold of your stirrup leathers and give a hard pull – they take a

9 THE RIGHT WAY OF GOING

One of the most important things about a show horse or pony, whether it be a Thoroughbred show hack, a Dales pony or an Arab, is that it must give its rider – and, where applicable, the judge – a good ride. The most breathtaking conformation and paces will not give you the winner's rosette – and the paces will not even show – if the animal pulls, naps or leans on the rider's hands.

Although good conformation and movement makes it theoretically easier for a horse to be a comfortable, balanced ride, it doesn't happen as if by magic. Correct schooling and riding and ring experience all play vital roles: when you see top exhibitors cantering effortlessly round the ring as if they haven't a care in the world, you can be sure that they've put in hours of work at home.

A lot of people equate the well-schooled show horse with the successful dressage horse, but there is a difference. Both must be responsive and obedient, but whilst the dressage horse has only to go well for its rider, the show horse must also give the judge a good ride. Basically, the show horse must go at whatever pace the rider dictates in a balanced, comfortable way. It need not be 'on the bit' to the same degree as the dressage horse, but it must be in self carriage. Above all, it must be a pleasure to ride: when you see a judge going round the ring with a big smile, you know you're in with a chance.

However, obedient does not mean brain dead. All judges accept that horses and ponies are not machines and that if you want sparkle and presence, you are not going to find yourself riding a police horse. This may apply particularly to hacks and any other horses which are full Thoroughbred or have a large percentage of Thoroughbred or Arab blood. Stereotyping is dangerous, but if you have to make generalizations, it is probably fair to say that a sensitive horse demands a calm, sensitive, confident rider. There are plenty of cobs who have their fair share of sparkle and often a sense of

Make sure your horse is used to being ridden by other people before you take him in the ring

Patient and varied
schooling at home
perfects a show
horse's way of going

the horse instantly by 'giving' the moment he responds to its action, are usually better than, for instance, draw reins. In the hands of an expert, draw reins may be fine, but we don't all have the finesse of, say, John Whitaker and if you are too late to release the rein you can't blame the horse for wondering what on earth you do want him to do.

The Pessoa lungeing system is another favourite and although it might look complicated, is simple to use. Like all the good training aids, it is helpful when used effectively, and if used ineffectively, won't do any harm! Again, the horse learns that if he puts his back end underneath himself and comes round in front, he puts himself in the most comfortable and effective position.

EXPERT VIEWS

With the little ponies, we lunge and long rein them to get them used to working and going off the voice. We might do a little lateral work – though not a lot – on the long reins and we'll do a bit of cantering on the lunge to get them going off the voice. It's important that they are relaxed and responsive to voice commands.

We're very keen on varying their routine and keeping it fun, for both ponies and riders. We hack them out, do a bit of work on the gallops and make the most of the fact that we've got a decent hill out the back! We don't gallop too much, it's more of a fun thing and the ponies are worked together periodically: just two or three

One of Lynn Russell's novice cobs being worked on a Pessoa lungeing system

together. You need to get the children confident, because if they aren't confident going into the ring they won't do their best.

I also love riding and judging Arabs – and the wonderful thing about Arabs is that it doesn't matter how badly they've been ridden, if you get on them and say 'Let's do it' they'll give you a lovely light ride – as a breed, they have a fantastic natural cadence. Unfortunately, a lot of the time people strap them down instead of using their legs and asking them to work correctly from behind.

The trouble with Arabs that have been shown in-hand in the 'head in the air' way is that you have to rehabilitate them to get them going well under saddle. Chambon work is very good for this, because it works them through the topline without any restriction from the rider's weight. When I'm judging in-hand classes, I tell people to stand them up like normal horses, not with their heads in the air so I can't see conformation. Nor do I accept that you have to have a plastic bag tied to the end of a stick and wave it around to get your horse's attention – you're not conducting the Philharmonic, you're showing a breed that has natural presence and charisma without the need for gimmicks.

Penny Hollings

Deciding when a young horse is ready to go out is really a matter of being able to assess how it's going at home. Youngsters tell you when they're ready – they've got to be happy in their work at home and give you the feeling that they're confident to do what you ask.

We vary our horses' work to keep them interested. We're lucky where we live in Norfolk, as we can hack a mile to a grass field we use and we've got green lanes where, when the going's good, you can trot and canter and pretend you're in the show ring. Our novices hack out with others and get used to working with other horses; they learn to work with things going on around them almost without realizing.

The really important thing is to get them working at home so that they're totally relaxed, but at the same time in front of your leg and going forward. When they get to a show they rely on you to give them confidence and if you've built this up at home, hopefully they know they can trust you.

Allister Hood, show producer

Although we have a school and use it as part of the horses' education, they hack out and are ridden in the fields as well. The important thing is that even when they're hacking, they are still working – they walk out properly, rather than just slopping along, and if I ask a horse to halt or make a transition I want an instant response, not when it's finished gawking at something in the hedge.

Intersperse schooling with hacking to keep your horse relaxed and interested in life.

I'll also ride horses in the field where others are turned out, so that they learn to listen to me in potentially distracting circumstances. Obviously I pick my horses, I don't want to get mown down by a galloping herd of four-year-olds!

One thing a lot of people fall down on is that they don't teach their horses manners. When you're judging, you expect a show horse to be bright and full of presence, and you would make allowances if, for instance, a horse in a novice class had a look if someone at the ringside suddenly put up an umbrella as it went past. But you don't expect to see horses in open classes napping

185

when asked to leave the line-up, or hanging towards the other horses when going past it.

If you're a one-horse owner, remember to get other people to sit on it sometimes – and if it's only ever been ridden by a woman, make sure it's been ridden by a man before it goes in the ring so it doesn't go badly or throw a wobbly the first time a heavier male judge gets on. In the same way, get someone to give you a leg-up on to it now and again. It's too easy to just get on and ride every day at home and then find the horse getting spooked when the judge and steward walk over to it prior to the steward giving the judge a leg-up.

Lynn Russell

To get the most out of native ponies, you have to think like one! You can't be forever riding them in circles in a school, because they'll get bored and find other things to amuse themselves with. I do most of my schooling out hacking, with short sessions on our flat bit in the field.

Julia Woods

Mountain and moorland working hunter classes are highly competitive

Jumping

Working hunter, hunter pony and cob classes have become increasingly popular and the standard is much higher than it used to be. Your aim should be to jump a flowing, fault-free round out of a good rhythmic canter – and the best way to achieve this is through a mixture of gridwork and competition experience.

Gridwork increases a horse or pony's athleticism and confidence as long as the person building the grid knows what he or she is doing. Your best bet is to find a good show jumping or working hunter specialist who can build grids appropriate for your horse or pony's experience and/or weaknesses and to combine this with some show jumping experience.

However well your horse jumps through a grid, he needs practice round courses. Before you enter your first working hunter, you should be jumping confidently and hopefully clear round show jumping courses of the same height; most regularly successful competitors start their horses and ponies off by jumping indoors through the winter.

Although these competitions are theoretically centred on courses of natural fences, the definition of natural varies from one course builder to another. Hazards of the past few years have ranged from wooden sheep to plastic ducks floating in the water! Be prepared to meet everything from water to bullfinches in the ring and where possible, build fences at home to simulate the problems they pose. These do not have to be grand – a bullfinch can be introduced by sticking a few twigs into an ordinary bush filler, building up the number as the horse gains confidence, whilst a safely weighted down strip of plastic makes a good imitation water hazard.

EXPERT VIEW

The worker, whether it is a working hunter, cob or hunter pony, must go as well on the flat as any other show horse. It's especially important that it is responsive to the leg and doesn't drop behind the bit, so that it can take you forward the instant you need to go.

Although show jumping – and lessons with a good show jumping trainer – is very useful for the worker, there are differences in what is expected of them. Show jumpers often work their horses in draw reins and concentrate on canter work without bothering too much about the trot. I don't work anything in draw reins, because I want a horse to be going from my leg into my hand, not off the bit, and do as much work in trot as the other paces – a worker needs to show a decent trot, because it's a show horse.

Show jumping specialists also want flying changes right from the start and teach their horses that every time they change direction, they automatically change their

Gridwork helps improve a working hunter's technique: Kate Moore on Mountain Road.

Working hunters have to cope with hazards such as bullfinches. Introduce these by putting thin branches in the side of fillers and gradually increasing the thickness and density as the horse gains confidence

canter lead. I do very little deliberate teaching of flying changes – the novices can come back to trot and with the open horses, who are expected to show them, I find that as the horses become balanced, the changes come naturally.

Gridwork is vital and I do it with all my horses. Different grids, with someone knowledgeable on the ground to help you change the distances, can correct a lot of novicey problems. For instance, if a horse does not have enough lift in front, then three oxers with a stride between each fence will help to improve its technique. I also work a lot on shortening and lengthening the canter stride so that the horse gets used to altering the length of the stride whilst keeping its rhythm.

Some of the distances in workers' classes are quite long, so they have to learn to respond if you sit and push in the middle of a combination. The courses aren't as easy as they look – some of the show jumpers reckon they are too simple, but if they ride them, they often find the reality is a bit different. You also get awkward lines of fences.

Workers need to be brave and I find that real hunting helps with that. I just wish we were in good post and rail country! We also take ours cross country-schooling and to hunter trials, but you won't see me galloping round a hunter trials course trying to win – I'll be schooling them at the pace I'll be going in the ring.

Kate Moore works Teddy Boy in the open and up and down slopes – a working hunter has to be confident going on

I also take them indoor jumping in the winter. Horses and riders can find it quite difficult, because the distances are shorter and the fences come up so quickly. But it's good for both of us, because it teaches horse and rider to be sharp.

A lot of people think that a good show jumper will automatically make a good worker, but that isn't the case. You need a bold horse that will go when you ask it, whereas a top class show jumper is ultra careful and might need to be placed exactly right at every fence. A worker should jump, and make a good job of it, as long as it's in more or less the right place.

Kate Moore

Schooling for side-saddle

Although most horses can be schooled to go side-saddle, for the showing game you are talking mainly about the ladies' hunter. There are exceptions – notably, Lynn Russell has won the prestigious Horse & Hound British Isles showing championship at Royal Windsor on the heavyweight show cob, Polaris – but they are few and far between. The big difference between showing classes and the side-saddle equitation classes run under the auspices of the Side Saddle Association is that in showing, it is the horse who is judged and in side-saddle equitation, it is the rider who comes under scrutiny.

That said, there are common denominators. In both cases, the horse must be a well-mannered, well-schooled ride and both horse and rider must be correctly turned out. A ladies' hunter who is too bouncy or who throws his head in the air will not find favour and in both disciplines, the overall picture must be of perfect elegance.

If you want to learn to ride side-saddle to compete in ladies' classes, you have to decide between learning from scratch on a horse you hopefully already know and trust or learning on an experienced horse before introducing your own to the art. A confident, positive rider may be able to learn along with her horse as long as she has the help of an experienced teacher, but many people find that it is best to have a few lessons or an intensive course on a schooled horse before having a go on their own animal.

The other advantage of this method is that it gives you the chance to make sure you are going to enjoy this approach before you invest a lot of money. A good secondhand side-saddle bearing a respected name such as Owen, Champion and Wilton or Mayhew will cost about £1500 whilst the latest model, designed by Roger Philpot, Side Saddle Association vice chairman and Desmond O'Brien, master saddler to the Spanish Riding School, will be about £2000. Add a few hundred more for a habit made from good quality cloth and it soon becomes an expensive pastime.

For a horse to go well side-saddle it must be responsive and forward thinking; you can't sit and kick. It must also have a good mouth and be guaranteed – as far as is possible – not to rear. A side-saddle puts the rider in such a secure position that it makes it difficult for her to fall off. This is a bonus for most of the time, but if a horse goes up and comes over backwards, such security means she is more likely to be trapped underneath it.

EXPERT VIEWS

A side-saddle is much heavier than an ordinary one, so I would not introduce it until the horse is six or seven. By then its muscles should be fully developed and it should have a strong back.

To give a good ride, it must be light off the leg and go forward into a contact, not drop the bridle and come back at you. When you start schooling a horse to go sideways you need to carry a schooling whip as a substitute for your right leg, so it must accept a light tap from this as readily as a leg aid.

The extra weight and the balance strap mean that a side-saddle feels different to the horse than an ordinary one, so you have to give it time to get used to it. When I put a side-saddle on for the first time, I girth it up and tighten the balance strap just enough so that the horse can feel it. I then lead him in both directions, gradually tightening the balance strap until I feel it's secure enough. This is where it is so vital for your saddle to be correctly fitted, so you don't need to over tighten the balance strap to try and keep it in place.

I like to lunge a horse in a side-saddle before I ride him to make sure he's happy to bend right and left. Whatever I'm doing, leading, lungeing or riding, I start on the right rein; this makes it easier for the horse because of the way a side-saddle distributes your weight.

Once he's happy on the lunge, I'll get a helper to leg me up – some people like to be legged up to sit astride first of all, then swing their right leg over, but I always go straight into the sideways position and have never had any problems. We then set off in walk, on the right rein, of course, and go on from there as his confidence increases.

If the rider is confident, so should the horse be. You've got to be able to keep him going forward, which means using your leg, the schooling whip and – very important – your voice.

Working a horse under side-saddle can actually improve his way of going astride. I had one show horse who naturally went on his forehand and was very difficult to lighten, but when I put a side-saddle on him it was much easier to get him to engage his hocks and lighten in front. The benefits carried through when I rode him astride again, as he had learned to carry himself.

It's very important to get a specialist to fit and do any adjustments on your side-saddle. Someone who is knowledgeable about fitting an ordinary one won't necessarily know how to fit a side-saddle.

Kate Moore

You can ride any type of horse side-saddle as long as it has the right conformation. I look for a good front and shoulder, a back that is not too short - because of the extra length of the side-saddle - and a comfortable stride. Because you're sitting to the horse all the time, you don't want anything with a short, choppy stride.

The biggest problem you're likely to find with a broad horse, particularly a cob, is getting a side-saddle to fit. When the original ones were made, they were made for narrower, Thoroughbred types, not modern hunters and cobs.

Lynn Russell

LAST WORD

You've done all the work at home and your horse or pony looks a picture. Now it's time to get out there in the real world – but you need to make sure that first experiences are good ones, for both of you.

One of the best ways of preparing a novice horse for the show ring is to take him to a couple of shows before you compete and simply ride him round to get used to all the sights and sounds. This means that neither of you are under pressure and he can be introduced to everything from loudspeakers to horses working in close proximity. Horses who have been shown in-hand two or three times as youngsters usually remember what it's all about, though you can't afford to be blasé and you need to make sure that your brakes and steering are established before taking a novice to introductory outings under saddle.

Travelling and working in on the showground are all part of the experience. This is where the horse who has been lightly shown in-hand will often be easier to deal with, as he should have become accustomed to travelling and to coping with the showground environment. If your horse has not travelled before, take him on a couple of short journeys first, perhaps with a sensible companion so that he can get used to it all.

EXPERT VIEWS

When we go to shows we often take youngsters along just for the experience. We usually take the four-year-olds to two or three just to ride round so that they get used to all the sights and sounds and to standing on the lorry.

You've got to know your showground. For instance, Ardingly is a good one for me – it's busy at the main end, but there's plenty of room at the other, so you can start at the quiet end and gradually let them see more of what's happening as they settle. We travel them in bandages with tape over the top and leave these on to work them in. This means you don't have to fiddle about when they might be a bit excited, but their legs are protected. I'll ride them in the tack they work in at home, plus a standing martingale so I've got a neckstrap if I need it!

Once a youngster has worked in and I'm sure its brain is between its ears, I ride round past the trade stands and stop and chat to people so the horse gets used to standing. If it's spooky, I'll hack it around with an experienced horse who is there competing and has seen it all before.

When a young horse is happy with it all, maybe even a bit bored, I'll enter it for its first class. I like early shows for youngsters, because they tend to be at venues without too many trade stands and occupational hazards such as parachutists falling out of the sky. I'll start with a small show in February – I have a favourite indoor venue – then one or two in March and the same in April. As you carry on, you have to be careful about the ground; if it's too hard, I'll leave them at home, because you don't want to put too much strain on their limbs.

Lynn Russell

When I've got a novice pony starting its first season, I don't actually start off with a showing show. I'll go to a small dressage competition, riding club show or even clear round jumping competition instead – you've only got to walk, trot and canter to do a Prelim dressage test and I'm not out to win, just to give the pony experience.

Julia Woods

When it's time for the real thing, your priorities are to be organized and to stay calm. Don't leave it until the last minute to discover, for instance, that the stitching is coming undone on your show bridle. Make sure that any documentation you need, such as a vaccination certificate, is ready to take and if you haven't been to the showground before, plan your route. Allow plenty of time to get there and aim to arrive at least an hour before your class is due to start so that you can collect your number, find out where your ring is situated and get your horse settled and working nicely.

Even the quietest horse or pony may come off the ramp at his first show looking as if his eyes are popping out of his head. This is where the experience and confidence of the rider is important, knowing when to let him look and when to say that it is time to work.

EXPERT VIEW
A lot of people like to lunge an excited horse before they get on it, but it's up to you to find a place where you won't get in other competitors' way. You can't expect other

riders to tiptoe around you, because they are too busy concentrating on their own horses, so if yours is about to perform airs above the ground, pick a quiet corner away from the main area to start with.

If you want to lunge, do it off the bit, not off a headcollar or cavesson. You've got to have control and the best way to do that is to pass the lunge line through the inside bit ring, over the head and clip it to the outside. Keep the horse going forwards, because if he's going forwards he's less able to throw a wobbly.

All you're trying to do on the lunge is take the edge off him, not tire him out, so as soon as you can, get on him. Stick to your quiet area and again, keep him going forwards so he's less likely to buck or mess about. If you stay calm and positive, it will hopefully rub off on him! You don't need to get heavy with a young horse, but by insisting that he listens to you, you are actually giving him confidence – you're reminding him of the work he does at home.

Lynn Russell

In the ring

After a couple of acclimatization shows, you should be ready for your first competitive outing. Ringcraft, the art of being in the right place at the right time and catching the judge's eye for all the right reasons, is a matter of skill, common sense and practice. Here are some tips from the professionals to help you make the most of your horse and pony – and avoid some common pitfalls!

- Arrive at the collecting ring in plenty of time, so that you can work in and enter the ring in a calm, positive way. This also gives you the chance to check out the opposition! When the steward calls the class forward, let a few riders go in front of you so your novice gets a lead in to the ring. Try not to position yourself immediately behind an animal that is much better/more established than yours, or it will make the contrast even greater. Similarly, try and avoid getting too close to anything that has shown signs of playing up!

- You are on show from the minute you walk in, so make sure that your horse's walk is purposeful without being hurried and that he is tracking up well. This is where first impressions are made.

- Keep an eye on the steward all the time. When you are given the signal to trot on, don't panic and rush your horse so he falls into an unbalanced shambles – and don't trot so fast that you push him out of his natural rhythm. Similarly, when the steward gives you the signal to canter, ask for your strike-off out of a corner,

Keep an eye on the steward, who will give instructions to change the rein or pace or come in to the centre of the ring

Keep your distance from the horse or pony in front

Stand your horse or pony so the judge can assess his conformation easily

Keep your horse balanced as you change the rein

Lynn Russell keeps
Apollo beautifully
balanced as she
accelerates

which will encourage the correct bend and correct lead. If your horse strikes off
on the wrong leg, keep calm, come back to trot, rebalance the horse and ask again
- Keep enough space between you and the rider in front. If you find you are being
held up, create your own space by circling away or going as deep into the corners
as you can without unbalancing your horse. Don't cut in front of other exhibitors
– this is bad manners and will not endear you to them or to the judge.
- Stay alert and make sure your horse does, too. Even if you are not pulled in near
the top when the judge makes a first line-up, don't assume you are out of the
reckoning.
- If you've entered a workers class and find that the course is too much for your
novice horse or pony's standard of schooling, withdraw. It's better to have nothing
to show for your entry fee than to risk your horse losing confidence or injuring
himself.
- Whatever happens, keep smiling!

Your horse must learn to stand quietly in the line-up – and leave it willingly

What every judge wants to see – a top show horse, beautifully ridden and presented and going in perfect balance.

As the season progresses, you will find out more about your horse or pony and whether or not he is going to live up to your expectations. Take a tip from Lynn Russell and keep a showing diary in which you can record results, judges' comments, how long it took to get to the showground and so on. Learn from your experiences, both good and bad, and you'll be able to look forward to next season with even more enjoyment.

Manners matter

Although showing is meant to be enjoyable, whether you are an amateur or a professional rider, both you and your horse are inevitably under pressure. Good behaviour is an essential attribute not just for the show horse, but for its rider and everyone associated with it – and whilst it's easy to stay smiling when things are going well, it's just as important to behave correctly when they don't work out as you had hoped.

In the ring, your job is to show off your horse or pony to its best advantage without getting in the way or compromising the safety of anyone else. That means everything from not getting too close to the horse in front to not blocking the judge's view of other riders, either accidentally or deliberately. A judge might forgive a mistake but will definitely not be impressed by a rider who deliberately tries to unsettle or cover up another competitor.

Watch the top riders and see how they are always thinking ahead so they can use the ring space. You never see them suddenly find themselves with nowhere to go, simply because they know how to create more space for themselves by riding into the corners of the ring and avoiding potential rugby scrums. Use your wits, don't just follow the herd!

Keeping your wits about you means being alert for a judge's instructions, which will be issued through his or her steward. If the judge asks you a question when you're standing in line, answer politely and briefly. In classes where the judge rides, you may be offered a comment on your horse's way of going – don't argue if you don't agree and don't expect a judge to ride a horse which has never been sat on by a rider who is larger/smaller/the opposite sex from you.

At the end of the day, when you enter a showing class you put forward your animal for a judge's opinion. If you don't share that opinion, you must smile politely and bear it. If you're puzzled about the judge's decision or want to know how he or she thinks you could improve, wait until the end of the class and then ask the steward if you could have a quick word with the judge. Most will be happy to chat as long as you ask in the right way and pick the right time to do it.

If you have a genuine complaint, follow the correct procedures for making an objection as laid down by the relevant showing body – at larger shows – or as laid down in the schedule. You may have to be prepared to put your money where your mouth is, in that you may be required to lodge a fee which will be refunded if your objection is upheld. The reasoning behind this is that it discourages people from making fatuous complaints whilst ensuring that genuine objections are heard.

You also need to ensure that your helpers and supporters are on their best behaviour. Grooms going into the ring should be smart and tidy and be careful not to get in the way of the judge, steward or other competitors. Standards have slipped over the past few years and many judges are finding it necessary to be stricter about what they expect: this is not simply a case of courtesy, but of safety. In a large class at a major show last year, one groom walked into the ring in front of a mounted ride judge and only the judge's quick thinking and reactions prevented the hapless helper from being mown down.

Ringside judging is part of the fun, but make sure your supporters do it without making disparaging remarks about either the judge or the other competitors. Top National Hunt trainer Terry Biddlecombe tells a funny but salutary story about an occasion when his wife, Henrietta Knight – not only a leading trainer but a consummate horsewoman and respected judge – was assessing a class of Connemara ponies, which she breeds and is an authority on. Terry stood at the ringside beside three ladies who loudly condemned Hen's choice and agreed that she had picked the 'wrong' pony – in other words, not the one belonging to their friend. They were mortified when she walked over at the end of the class and they realised they had been standing next to her husband!

THE JUDGES' VIEWS

I do find it sad that manners have become much more slipshod – and I have to say that it isn't always riders who are at fault. At one of our major shows competitors were less than impressed when a judge was munching away on a hamburger whilst he was assessing conformation; it wasn't so much that he was eating, but the implication that he wasn't giving his full attention to the horses in front of him. I also think it's discourteous not to watch the whole of a rider's individual show; occasionally you'll see a judge turn away before the rider has finished, when courtesy demands an acknowledgement.

Having said that, some competitors get very cross if the judge doesn't ride all the animals in the line-up. I appreciate that everyone pays the same entry fee and deserves the same 'value for money,' but large shows in particular have to run to a timetable and if not riding a few horses at the bottom of the line isn't going to affect placings, there may be occasions when you have to finish the class without riding every animal. If it hasn't gone well enough for its rider to impress you, it isn't going to undergo a sudden transformation just because you get on it.

Also, and this is very important, a surprising number of riders don't understand exactly why the judge rides the horses. You are not there to school them, you are there to see if they give you a correct, balanced ride. I remember one class in particular where a horse behaved appallingly in the ring and the rider appeared to have very little control. Rather than ask permission to take it out of the class, which she should have done, she was determined to get her money's worth.

As she stood in line, she cheerfully told my steward that she was looking forward to me riding her horse because so far, she was the only person who had sat on it! My steward discreetly passed this on to me and I declined to ride it. Although she didn't say anything in the ring, the lady asked me afterwards in a very indignant way why I hadn't ridden her horse; when I told her that riding it wouldn't have affected the placings and that I wasn't there to school it, she said it wasn't fair and how else was it to get experience? I'm afraid that by then, my patience was wearing rather thin!

Not that long ago, grooms would not be allowed in the ring unless wearing a shirt, tie, hat and jacket. That unspoken rule has relaxed somewhat, but it should surely be a compliment to the judge, the show organisers and the competitor you are grooming for to be smartly turned out, with a hat – not wearing shorts and a boob tube, as I've seen on plenty of occasions.

I know that these days, most grooms are family members and friends who do it for love. But if you don't want to annoy the judge – or get squashed – please dress smartly, don't go in to 'your' horse until the judge has ridden it, take an appropriate route in and out of the ring and don't take a shopping trolley full of grooming kit with you.

When you're judging, a good steward can make your job easier and more enjoyable – and a bad one can be a nightmare. I know most stewards are volunteers, but so are judges, and whilst everyone has to learn, you do need to appreciate what the job entails. As a judge, you are the person responsible for the safe conduct of a class; your steward is there to assist you in enabling it to run as smoothly as possible, not to influence your decision or tell you how to do things.

One thing I hate is when a steward tries to give me a running commentary on the animals in my class, telling me who placed it where, who bred it and so on. This may come from a desire to be helpful, but I really don't want to know. I judge horses as I see them on that day and it doesn't bother me if a horse I haven't placed was champion last time out.

Having said all that, it would be a really good idea if everyone who showed horses had to do a couple of stints stewarding. They would then realise how difficult it is to keep things running smoothly and how annoying it is when riders don't pay attention to what's going on.

In general, children in the ring today have good manners – in some cases, better than their parents'! Two things annoy me intensely: one is children who cry if they don't win and the other is parents who march up to their children as they leave the ring and start berating them because they make a mistake or didn't ride as well as they should have done. Come to that, maybe that's why some of them cry...

In pony classes, I always watch every child's show and think it is important to acknowledge each one with a smile. Similarly, I try and have a word with each one and offer encouragement to those who aren't placed. It takes very little time and I do think it makes a difference to little riders. I will always remember the little girl at the bottom of the line who gave me a beaming smile when I said her pony was well-behaved and announced that she wouldn't swap him for any of the others!

Judges and judging

Judging show animals is so subjective that decisions will sometimes be made that upset the applicant. As one well-known judge puts it, at the end of any class you will have one satisfied rider and a lot more not-so-satisfied ones. However, although individual preferences and priorities will always come into play, judges have a responsibility to be as fair as possible.

Instances which cast doubt on the judging process do occur and it is important that judges are aware of the rules of all the relevant societies and are aware of circumstances which could leave their decisions vulnerable to criticism. For instance, they must be extremely careful not to leave themselves open to accusa-

A winning smile from Lynn Russell – the red rosette is the reward for hours of hard work

tions of favouring particular animals or riders because of personal connections or other considerations.

There have, of course, been high profile cases of judges being 'disciplined' by ruling bodies for contravening rules. Whatever the rights and wrongs of a complicated subject, it is generally accepted that a judge who does not follow the rules of the body he or she is judging for, even if this happens accidentally, has failed in his or her responsibility.

No one wants witch hunts, or to get to the stage where judges become an endangered species because people are frightened to take on the responsibility. What every genuine showing enthusiast wants is a fair deal for all: exhibitors, judges and officials. And you can't say fairer than that!

USEFUL CONTACTS

British Show Hack, Cob and Riding Horse Association

You need to be a member and to register your horse if you compete in any of these categories at larger shows affiliated to the association.

BSHCRHA, Chamberlain House, Chamberlain Walk, 88 High Street, Coleshill, Birmingham B46 3BZ

Tel: 01675 466211, fax: 01675 466242. e-mail: bshcrha@cdosgroup.com

Website: www.osborne-ref.co.uk

Sport Horse Breeding (GB)

Governing body for all in-hand and ridden hunter classes at major shows.

SHB(GB), 96, High St, Edenbridge, Kent TN8 5AR.

Tel: 01732 866277, fax: 01732 867464.

Website: www.sporthorsegb.co.uk

National Pony Society

Organizes annual show with variety of classes and society championships, national championships wih finals held at important events at the end of the season and affiliation scheme to encourage classes for registered riding ponies and mountain and moorland breeds.

NPS, Willingdon House, 102, High St, Alton, Hants GU34 1EN

Tel: 01420 88333, fax 01420 80599

Website: www.nationalponysociety.org.uk

British Show Pony Society

Promotes classes for show ponies, show hunter ponies and working hunter ponies, including lead rein, 158cm and heritage mountain and moorland classes. All affiliated shows qualify for the summer or winter champonships.
BSPS, 124, Green End Road, Sawtry, Huntingdon, Cambs PE28 5XS.
Tel: 01487 831376, fax 01487 832779
Website: www.britishshowponysociety.co.uk

Ponies Association (UK)

Provides a range of events throughout the UK covering all disciplines and stages its own shows.
Ponies Association (UK), Chesham House, 56 Green End Road, Sawtry, Huntingdon, Cambs PE28 5UY.
Tel: 08700 785 123, fax 01487 832086, e-mail info@poniesuk.org
Website: www.poniesuk.org

Coloured Horse and Pony Society

Promotes all aspects of the coloured horse and pony. Holds qualifiers for the Horse of the Year Show, pony qualifiers for the PNPS and BSPS championship shows and its own CHAPS UK championship show and stallion and mare gradings.
HAPS UK, 1, McLaren Cottages, Abertysswg, Rhymney, Tredegar NP22 5BH.
Tel/fax 01685 845045
Website: www.chapsuk.com

British Skewbald and Piebald Association

Promotes all aspects of the skewbald and piebald horse and pony. This year sees its first qualifiers for a championship at the RIHS, also has a full range of shows throughout the UK and a two-day World Championships of Colour show. Holds stallion and mare gradings.
BSPA, PO Box 67, Ely, Cambs CB7 4FY
Tel: 01474 700038, fax 01354 638238, show helpline 01354 638123

Joint Measurement Board

Joint Measurement Board, PO Box 322, Horley RH6 OWS

Tel: 01293 862101

Members include the BSHCRHA, BSPS, NPS, Ponies Association (UK) and Sport Horse Breeding (GB). Appoints official measurers, all veterinary surgeons, who measure animals on approved measuring pads using measuring sticks that have been certified by Trading Standards weights and measures departments.

The Side Saddle Association

Promotes all aspects of side-saddle riding and keeps a register of instructors.

The SSA, Woodlands, Broadbury, Oakhampton, Devon EX20 4NH

Tel: 01837 871313

INDEX

211